Showmanship in Public Speaking

Books by Edward J. Hegarty

HOW TO RUN A SALES MEETING
BUILDING A SALES TRAINING PLAN
HOW TO RUN A MEETING
HOW TO WRITE A SPEECH
SHOWMANSHIP IN PUBLIC SPEAKING

Showmanship

IN PUBLIC SPEAKING

Edward J. Hegarty

McGRAW-HILL BOOK COMPANY, INC.

New York London Toronto

SHOWMANSHIP IN PUBLIC SPEAKING

Library of Congress Catalog Card Number: 51-13607

FOURTH PRINTING

Published by the McGraw-Hill Book Company, Inc.

PRINTED IN THE UNITED STATES OF AMERICA

To my mother

who thinks anything I write is good

Preface

In towns and cities all over the United States, every weekday in the year, doctors, lawyers, and merchants rush out of their offices about noon to go to a luncheon meeting. The club bulletin has told them about today's speaker. It said he would be good, plenty good. And so there is some hope among these men as they hurry to their appointed places. Not too much hope, but some. They know about the veal chop with tomato sauce; they know about the potatoes, the vegetables, and the dessert. But the speaker—he is the unknown in the equation. As the member hurries to get in under the bell, he wonders, "Will this fellow be good?"

The same question is in the minds of thousands of other listeners in women's clubs, civic organizations, sales meetings, conventions. They are all hoping that today's speaker will be different, that he will do something or say something that the speaker last week didn't do or say. They are not looking for much—just one idea, perhaps, or a story they can tell.

To all these listeners, speakers fall into four categories:

1. The speaker who says nothing and puts on no show
2. The speaker who says something and puts on no show
3. The speaker who says nothing and puts on a good show
4. The speaker who says something and puts on a good show

The last two are the kinds that listeners like. A speaker can say nothing, yet make a good talk if his show compensates for what he didn't say. You can check this yourself. Next time you hear a good speech, ask yourself, "What did the speaker say?" You may find that you can't recall one constructive point. Yet, because he put on a good show, you felt that he made a good speech. Of course, the best speaker is the one who says something and at the same time puts on a good show. The listener feels that he has hit the jackpot when he hears such a speaker.

This book tells how a speaker can improve his speeches with showmanship, how he can get into classes three and four. If you are going to speak to luncheon clubs, civic groups, sales organizations—in fact, if you are going to speak anywhere—you want to send your listeners home saying, "This fellow was good." And on top of that you want them to say, "He had a real message, too." If that is your ambition, try out some of the suggestions given on the following pages. Perhaps if enough speakers think enough about the show they put on, those long-suffering listeners will have a more pleasant life.

EDWARD J. HEGARTY

Contents

Showmanship in Public Speaking

I

Why Showmanship in Public Speaking?

Perhaps you never thought of that speech you made to the boys at the club as a show. Most speakers wouldn't. But think back now. Wasn't there quite a bit of showmanship connected with it?

When one friend heard that I was writing a book on showmanship in public speaking, he said, "But, Ed, I don't want to put on an act. I just want to make good speeches."

Maybe you don't want to put on an act, but how can you help it? One of my speaker friends says, "Being yourself when you are up before an audience calls for a bit of acting." Did you ever think of having to act to be yourself? But there are times when you have to do it. As the verse puts it,

With your knees a-knockin'
Your hands a-sweatin'
Your voice refusin' to work.

When you are in that spot, isn't some showmanship called for? Just to be yourself, to project your personality?

Such showmanship doesn't call for standing on your head, dancing a jig, working yourself into a frenzy, shouting for joy, or tearing your hair. When you are in the condition described by the verse, you need showmanship just to stand up and smile.

You may say, "But I am never nervous when I stand up to face an audience. I don't shake or sweat or have trouble speaking."

Fine, but you do put on a freshly pressed suit that day, don't you? And why do you put on the light-gray suit with the white shirt and the bright-red necktie? Don't you select that outfit because it makes a better show than the dark-gray tweed and the green tie?

Then, when you get to your feet after the chairman's introduction, why don't you slouch or lean on the lectern? Don't you stand erect because you want to impress these listeners?

Next, when you speak, why do you use the tone of voice, the volume, the intensity you do? Isn't it because you are trying to show the conviction you feel?

Yes, everything you do before an audience is a part of a show —your appearance, your voice, your smile, all of it. You can't help it. Then isn't it a good idea to learn what you can do about this kind of showmanship?

Another comment I get is, "Ed, I never will be able to get up before a group and play a clown. I'm just a regular fellow."

Good, but let me ask this, "How many speakers have you heard lately that impressed you as regular fellows?"

Not many, were there? And the ones that appeared to be regular fellows made good speeches, didn't they? But nevertheless the others, aren't they good fellows? Without doubt they are, for so often the speaker who acts like a stuffed shirt before an audience is regular to his friends and associates. Then why does he seem like a stuffed shirt when he is speaking? Isn't he putting on an act? Not the right act, I admit, but an act just the same.

Let's say you gave a businesslike talk before a business audience on a business subject that convinced the listeners that you were a sound businessman. The impression you left is partly the result of showmanship, isn't it? You dressed, talked, and acted like a businessman, and they accepted you as such. What you said had much to do with that impression, but your looks, your manner, and your attitude had as much or more to do with it.

What you said was your speech. What you showed those listeners—that's what I call your showmanship. And the showmanship left the impression. In some talks, showmanship may not call for one gesture or a single raising or lowering of the voice. But it does call for something more than what you say. So as you start these pages, don't think of showmanship as the flash of fireworks or the booming of cannon. The showmanship I plan to cover is in those things you do that help you leave the impression you want to leave.

Not long ago one of the young men in our sales-training course asked me, "How important do you consider this speaking work we are doing in class?"

"You attended our sales convention last month," I said. "Which of the young men on the program do you think knew his subject best?"

The young man mentioned three names.

"Do you think those fellows made the best talks?" I asked.

"Without a doubt," he said.

"How much do you think their speeches had to do with your impression of their over-all ability?" I asked.

"Well, I don't know," he admitted.

I then asked him to name the man who gave the impression that he had the most ability. He mentioned a name. "Do you know anything about this man's background?" I asked.

The boy knew little about the man's education, experience, or any other measure of his ability.

"Yet you think he is the most promising young man on the program?"

The boy agreed.

"Then doesn't that answer your question?" I asked. He knew nothing about the speaker, but the speaker's showmanship had greatly impressed him, just as your showmanship, when you speak, will impress your listeners.

When you speak to strangers, how can they judge you except by what you say and the show you put on? When you speak to a group you know, can they help measuring your ability by the kind of job you do on your feet? Perhaps it is not right, but that is how it is. You have two men with the same background of education, experience, and ability. Stand them up to speak, and they are a standoff as to looks and ability to wear clothes. But one is what you call a good speaker, and the other makes a poor impression. Which of the two will go ahead faster?

All my life I have worked in advertising, sales, promotion, and public relations. I have watched some young men rise, and others stay where they were or go back. Out of this experience I can say that the most important training a young man can get is in speaking well in public. That is true in almost any kind of work.

When you learn to speak in public, you develop your personality and your ability to make friends. Why is that? Well, to make a good speech you have to think of the listeners, don't you? And what's the number one characteristic of the people you don't like? They think too much of themselves, don't they. When you speak to a group you have to think of them, of their interests, of what your message means to them. If you don't, you won't give a good talk.

For some, learning to speak well to groups is a tough assignment. But it is not half as difficult as you may think it is. I can well remember the days when I broke out in a cold sweat at the thought that I might be called on. Not long ago as the guest speaker of the evening, I sat next to the president of the club. That night he had to read the club's annual report. "I have butterflies in my stomach," he said. "You know, this is my second year as president of this group, but I don't seem to get over it."

There is nothing strange about that. I am nervous before a talk, even with thousands of appearances behind me. But I need that nervousness. When I feel nervous, I tell myself that I am going to be good.

When I was a youngster, just starting in business, I was deathly afraid of getting on my feet to talk. Our sales department had dinners every month. At these dinners various men were called upon to talk. I seldom enjoyed the dinners. I sat through the speaking hoping that I would not be next. Then, one night I was asked to talk. As I got up to speak, the man next to me at the table moved to get out of my way. His foot caught in an electric cord. Just as I said, "Gentlemen," in a rather halting voice, there was a flash.

Every light in the room went out. The laugh was tremendous. When the lights came back on, the audience was still laughing, and some were calling suggestions. Encouraged, I went on and gave a good talk. The boss complimented me on it. He said, "We will use you in the next sales meeting."

They did, and they kept on using me. Even though I didn't know it, I could talk fairly well. I had had no training, but I bought a few books and studied what I was trying to do. Later, I took courses in speaking. Still later, I ran such courses.

I tell this story to illustrate the point that no matter how poorly you talk now, you can become good. I feel strongly about that. Of course, I assume that you know the subject you are to talk about. But haven't you noticed this? You have heard a speaker talk about a subject that had no interest for you, but somehow he holds your interest. How much of it is showmanship? Then you hear a man speak on a subject in which you are greatly interested; yet he does not interest you. Is it because he puts on a poor show? Both men may know the subject; but one of them knows how to stage his show, the other does not.

There are a lot of tricks to showmanship. Some speakers never seem to learn them, no matter how many talks they make. Now what is your reaction to a poor speaker? You feel he does not know his subject, don't you? If a speaker makes a good talk, you feel he knows his subject. Perhaps the difference between two speakers is that one knew the tricks, the other didn't. Then your judgment is not correct, is it? Should you judge a man's ability on his showmanship, on his knowledge of tricks of speaking?

The trouble is, you can't help it. It is natural for you to judge the man on that evidence. It is natural for everybody to do the same.

Well, if you are going to be judged on your showmanship, shouldn't you try to learn some of these tricks? I call them tricks, but maybe I should give them more dignity and suggest that you learn the procedures that good speakers use. How do I qualify to explain them? In the course of a year I listen to hundreds of speeches. While I listen to what men say, I watch what they do.

When a man does something in making a speech, I make notes on what he does and exactly how he does it. Then I check for the effect on his audience. Of course, I speak a lot myself—perhaps sixty to one hundred speeches each year before audiences of all kinds, large and small. In making these appearances, by cutting and trying, I have found out what goes over and what does not. So in this book you won't find too much about what great men say about the tricks of speechmaking, but you will find a lot of illustrations of how good speakers use their showmanship.

Let's say that you have to do a speech next month. You want this speech to be good, to do some good for you, for your company, or for the organization you represent. O.K., let's talk about what makes a good speech.

2

What Makes a Good Speech?

If you hadn't read Chap. 1, you might answer, "Material—good material."

And my reply would be, "Yes, you're close."

But now that you have read what went before, you know you have to know how to use the material. I covered the writing of a speech in my book *How to Write a Speech.* So let's assume that you have the speech written, you have the points firmly fixed in your mind, and you are all ready to stand up and give out. What now?

You hear a speech and you remember one point that the speaker made. Why is that? How did the speaker make that one point? Can you recall? If you are going to make good speeches, wouldn't it be a good idea for you to learn the devices used by good speakers so that you can use them yourself?

I have a speech called "How to Get Better." It is a talk selling the listener on why he should train himself to get better. There is nothing new in this talk. It is about things that all the people in the audience know—the smile, the ability to listen, the use of simple language that makes meaning clear. All of it is simple A-B-C stuff, but the talk goes over well. I have done it for small groups and for large audiences. In this talk I do a stunt that illustrates how it pays to listen with the eyes. I make the point that it pays to learn to listen. Then I say that I will give the audience a tip that will improve their listening tremendously. I suggest that they learn to listen with their eyes. I develop this point and then I give a demonstration. I ask the audience to look at me, all of them, all eyes on my eyes while I talk. When I get the attention of the group, all eyes on my eyes, I say, "Listen with your eyes; listen with your eyes; listen with your eyes." I say this slowly, and by the time I have said it three times the audience is quiet. I have complete attention. Then I say, "Notice how quiet it has become in this room? You can hear a pin drop. Nobody has moved; nobody has coughed; nobody has said a word; nobody has lighted a cigarette or anything." I let that sink in; then I button up my point. I say, "That's what happens when you listen with your eyes."

Not so long ago I did this demonstration before an audience of 6,500 persons in Los Angeles. I was in Los Angeles for about a week after that. I met a number of persons who had heard the speech and all of them mentioned this stunt. It was the one point that most of them took home.

That was gratifying, of course; my point had registered. But I asked a number of these men, "Could you describe just how I did that stunt?" Most of them tried, but out of perhaps twenty, only one could come close to describing what I had done. One out of twenty—not a good average, is it? And most of these men made talks themselves. They were salesmen or officers of groups. Yet, although what I had done had registered with them, how I had done it was wholly missed. Maybe that's why there is such a low average of good speakers.

Now what I will do here is to give you some suggestions as to how these things are done. These are things I learned in two ways—by observing and by doing. At times you may get the idea that I am trying to play up my accomplishments as a speaker when I relate my experiences. That's O.K. I am rather cocky about my speaking ability; my friends will tell you that.

However, while I will talk a lot about my own experiences, let me admit this. Most of the things that I do I have seen others do before me. Some of them I believe I have developed to a higher point than they have been done before. I have seen others do things I don't think I could do as well. But I have watched and I will tell you how they get the effects.

There is, of course, another reason for telling about my experiences. I lived through them. I enjoyed the successes; I felt the failures. Oh, yes, there were flops. Sometimes my material and my stunts fell down with a boom. Always I try to analyze why. At times I can; at others the reason escapes me. Perhaps my reasons may not be the real ones, but they are the result of some study; and I'll present them for what they may be worth to you.

Learning to be a good speaker is not too difficult. That is, if you are willing to work at it. After all, there are but a few speech elements. Learn to use some or all of them, and you can be an effective speaker. What is my list of these elements? Well, try this for size—the anecdote, news, dramatics, the demonstration, the stunt, the use of exhibits or speaking aids, and your language. As you look over that list, can you add any additional elements? Perhaps you can, but this list covers the main headings. What I plan to do is to take up these elements one by one and tell you what I have learned about them.

3

Your Four Big Problems

You have many problems when you make a speech, but here are the big four. Some speakers lick one of the problems, others two or three, but the good speaker covers all of them. Because they seem to be so little understood, I am listing them here in large type, so that as you read on you will keep them in mind. Here they are:

1. TRY TO MAKE OUT THAT YOU ARE A GOOD FELLOW
2. HOLD YOUR LISTENERS' INTEREST
3. KEEP ON YOUR OBJECTIVE
4. GIVE THEM SOMETHING TO TAKE HOME

Let's talk a little about each of them.

1. Try to Make Out That You Are a Good Fellow

The average speaker is introduced. He gets to his feet, he looks out over the audience, and what does he do? He scowls. Perhaps the poor fellow is nearsighted. It may be that he can't distinguish a face beyond the first row, but why the scowl? You say, "Oh, brother, another sourpuss."

You have seen the speaker who is stiff and formal when he stands to address you. He looks like a banker about to refuse a loan or a judge about to sentence the condemned. One look, and you have him pegged as a stuffed shirt. The fellow next to you whispers, "If he'd unbend, he'd crack." You think, "What he needs is a good swift kick." You know that you want none of his advice, good as it may be.

Then there is the speaker who is so much above you. He is superior; you know it from his manner. You are lucky to have him as your speaker. He is granting you a favor to be there at all. You wonder, "How does a guy get that way?" And you want little of him.

There is still another type that you see quite often—the speaker with the chip on his shoulder. From the first words, he is telling you, "Do this or else." He complains about the poor transportation facilities and about the bad hotel, and wonders why he ever came to a one-horse town like this. You wish you could tell him what to do about it, but. . . . You know you are not going to relish any of his advice.

You may say, "But, Hegarty, I am a sourpuss, I am stiff and formal, I am superior. Why shouldn't I act natural?" Let's say you are all of that. But look, some people like you, don't they? How about your wife and children, or those pals who take dimes from you at golf or gin? All I ask is that you show some of the stuff that makes these people like you.

When you are speaking to a group, you are an actor. If you are a sourpuss, you have to act as if you are not. If you are naturally stiff and formal with strangers, you have to give yourself that kick in the pants that causes you to unbend. If you think you are better than the listeners, hide your thoughts. If you are out there with a chip on your shoulder, don't let it show. It may take all your histrionic ability to cover up your natural liabilities, but it pays.

When you stand up before the group, you need that poise and balance that makes you one of them. You are a gentleman and scholar; you go to church on Sunday; there's a shine on the seat of your trousers; your children have no more respect for your opinion than their children have for theirs. You are friendly, courteous, and glad to talk to them. So put on your most pleasing personality and start in your most pleasant voice. You are all the introduction said, and with it you are a good fellow.

2. Hold Their Interest

Why did you doze off during that last talk at your luncheon club? "The speaker was no good," you say. But, why was he no good? Wasn't it because he didn't hold your interest? Well, if you don't hold their interest, why should they listen to you?

So lose no time in telling why it is to their interest to listen to you. The listener sits there asking, "What does it mean to me?" Tell him in words he can understand. A speaker says, "I'd like to tell you this. . . ." He should say, "You will be interested in this, and here is why."

All through that talk keep reminding the listener of what this subject means to him. If you are trying to get the group interested in building a new wing on the hospital, the civic pride of having a fine hospital may be an appeal for you, but you better try to make your appeal more personal. Perhaps, if this rich old duck could see himself in a bed in a ward or even in a hall because this wing was not built, he might be more inclined to cough up.

You can help hold this interest by the kind of material you use. Listeners like certain kinds of speech material. There are suggestions for speech material in this book. But no matter what kind of material you use, you still have the problem of slanting it. You have to tell me what it means to me. Tell me once, tell me twice, and then keep on telling me until you see my head nodding in agreement. If you don't hold my interest, why should I listen to you?

3. Keep on Your Objective

It isn't easy; at least, many speakers don't find it so. Too many seem to follow this plan: stand up; talk so long; sit down. You can get by with that. It is done every day. But when you speak, have a clear idea of what you are trying to do. If your purpose is to entertain or amuse, you can tell how you are doing by the laughs and the applause. But if you are trying to sell a bill of goods—and most speakers are—you should make sure that the audience gets the idea.

You no doubt have a number of points. Do you give each point the once-over-lightly treatment, or do you wrap it up in a neat package before you leave it? Do your points add up? Do they advance the main point? A speech is much like a road from one place to another. To go from one to the other, you have to stay on the road. How many speakers do that? They start all right, but then they get off on the side roads. In that way a speech is like a conversation. It can go from business to baseball in nothing flat. I have a friend who is a rambling speaker. He is a good speaker, he holds interest, he gets laughs; but you can't depend on him to sell an idea for you. His speeches cover so much territory that the listener has no clear idea of the points he makes. A man can make a good speech and not sell his deal. He misses because he rambles too far afield.

My plan for keeping on the beam is to do the speech in units. You may ask, "What do you mean, unit?" In my book, *How to Write a Speech,* I give a full explanation of the unit principle of organization. Here is a brief summary.

Suppose you have five points to make in this talk of yours. With the unit plan of speech organization you make the coverage of each point a speech in itself, perhaps a two- or three-minute speech.

Such a unit might be made up of these elements:

1. A statement of your premise
2. An anecdote that proves your point
3. A second statement of your premise

That would be the simplest kind of unit. With this type of organization you make your point three times—once in the original statement of the premise, again in the story, and a third time in the restatement.

In a more elaborate unit you might use any amount of material between the two statements of your premise. In my book *How to Write a Speech,* I offer this formula:

1. State your premise.
2. Quote an ancient—Marcus Aurelius, Cato, Homer. What did he say about the idea?

3. Quote a poet—Shakespeare, Emerson, Service, Riley. One of them said something close.
4. Quote the Bible.
5. Tell an anecdote about a famous character—Lincoln, F.D.R., Babe Ruth. Let it help prove the premise.
6. Now a story about an ordinary person—a bellhop, a taxi driver, a bartender. Again emphasize the premise.
7. Restate your premise, just in case the listeners have not got it yet.

That gives seven steps to the unit. The principle is the same as with the three-step unit; you have simply brought on more evidence. The steps in between the two statements can be filled with evidence, data, figures, news, or whatever you have.

Under the unit plan you cover each point completely. Each unit should be a speech in itself. Put the units together in the proper order and you have your twenty- or thirty-minute speech made up of short speeches.

Try out this unit idea; it will help keep you on your objective. You are out to do something with this speech. Keep trying to do that something from start to finish.

4. Give Them Something to Take Home

What right have you to take up the time of your listeners if you don't give them something in return? It may be an idea, a plan, or a work procedure. But give them something. Too many speeches leave nothing at all with the listener. The speaker covers a lot of ideas, but he leaves them dangling. Not long ago I was asked to go over a script for a speech. I read the script and suggested, "What you need is a summary. Why can't you give the listeners a three-step plan for doing this job?"

"Thanks, I never thought of that," the speaker said.

Now this man was an experienced speaker. He had given this talk a number of times, but he felt there was something wrong with it. Too many speakers are like this one. They don't realize that they haven't buttoned up. They leave the listener asking, "What does he want us to do?"

"I told them," the speaker says. And perhaps he did. But the telling is sometimes not enough. You have to tell them and tell them. You have to make sure that they understand.

"But I don't have a plan for them," you say. All right, you have an idea, don't you? Are you sure they understand what that idea is? After I do my talk "How to Get Better," listeners tell me, "You didn't give me anything new, but you reminded me of a number of things I should be doing." O.K., so they take home a reminder of what they should be doing. *They take something home.* In all your talks plan to give the audience something to take home. It will be better if, in that closing, you give them a summary of your gift to them.

As you read the following chapters of this book, try to keep these four problems in mind. You will find that many of the suggestions will help you on these problems.

4

Get Off to the Right Start

Smile!

That's right, Mr. Speaker—*Smile.*

Go all out; give it full steam; open your mouth; show your white teeth. Look at all corners of the room—beaming.

Yes, that is the way to start every speech—with a smile. Stand up and, while the group is applauding, smile at them.

When I start, I stand up slowly. I smile and I help them applaud. The action called for by my applause brightens my smile. I am not a man standing still smiling at them. I am a man in action smiling at them. Next time you look into a mirror, smile at yourself. Then start applauding, and see what happens to your smile—it broadens, takes on more life. My smile and my applause have just the right effect on that audience. They are supposed to be applauding me, and when they see a large, fat man smiling and applauding himself, it tickles them. And so their smiles widen and some of them laugh out loud. It is the kind of reception I want.

Make this smile you give the audience a real smile. Too many of us seem to be trying to suck on a lemon and smile at the same time. It can't be done. Tomorrow when you get up and look in the mirror, smile at yourself. Give yourself a real smile, just like the one you plan to give that audience. I'll bet that the smile you see can be improved. Try going all out with that smile. You are glad to be there, aren't you? Yes, even with your knees knocking you are glad to be there. So why not show it?

Usually when a speaker stands up to start his talk, he scowls out over the lights at his audience. Watch this in the next talk you hear. What is the speaker trying to do—scare the audience? There isn't a chance. If the speaker does venture a smile, note how he goes about it. It may be a half-smile, as if he doesn't know whether or not a smile is proper before this club.

Start with a smile. Stand and smile until they smile back at you. Usually it will take but a few seconds. There have been times when it was difficult to get the group to smile back at me. At a meeting not long ago I stood up and smiled at the group, and nobody smiled back. I stood there smiling, and still nobody went along. Then I laughed aloud, but that didn't do too much good. Then I turned to the chairman and asked, "What is this, a gag? Don't they know that I wrote a book in which I told speakers that if they stood up and smiled at an audience the audience would smile back at them? What are they trying to do—make a liar out of me?" You can be sure that by this time I had the group smiling with me.

Try it next time you make a speech. You'll get a big thrill out of watching your smile transfer itself to the faces of the group before you.

When you stand up, they'll probably have one of those speaking stands in front of you—a lectern. It is not to lean on. Try to stand up straight, with your chest out, as if you were on your toes, alive, ready to give it all you have. Get your hands in front of you but not on that lectern. It is a great temptation to hang onto that stand as if you would drop without its support; but forget it . . . pretend it isn't there . . . stand on your own two feet as if you were full of vim and vitality.

As you start, show your enthusiasm. No matter what your subject, try to get over to the group that to you this subject is important at this moment. I know this is a tough assignment, one of the toughest a man faces. But if you stand straight, smiling at them and radiating health, you will get off to a better start. So as the chairman makes the introduction, give yourself a pep talk. Say, "Get up and slay them; get up and slay them."

Then as you start, speak a bit louder than you think you need to talk. If there is a microphone, stand a bit away from it so that you can speak loudly without blasting. When you talk louder, you make yourself work harder, you throw more effort into what you say, and you seem to have more enthusiasm. If you seem steamed up about the subject, the group feels that it, too, should be interested. Always try to start a bit louder than the chairman finished. That is a good gauge. These people came here to hear you and you want to cooperate. Note how experienced speakers do this. They use all the tricks they know to capture attention right from the start.

You may say, "Wait a minute, Hegarty, I'm not an experienced speaker. I can't do these things you say." Is that so? Why can't you talk louder? Why can't you keep from leaning on the lectern? And you can smile, too, can't you? Nothing difficult about that.

O.K. then, let's say you are on your feet, standing straight, bubbling over with enthusiasm, your hands in front of you. What do you do now? Well, you have to say something. Most books on public speaking will tell you how to do this. Some say, "Wow them with that first sentence. Make it so strong that you kindle a flame, that you get them with you right at the start." Well . . . maybe you can do it. I never could.

Now my plan is to start on the low beat, easy, relaxed. After all, you have a number of things to do with your opening.

You have to convince the audience that you are a regular fellow.

You have to make them feel that you know your subject and that there is a logical reason why you should take up their time discussing it.

You have to get in good with them. You have to show that you are on their side . . . that your interests are their interests.

One scheme I use is to kid the management of the club about putting me on the program. I explain to the group that the chairman and the committee are sitting there worrying about me—they wonder if I will make a good talk. They are hoping, but they have their fingers crossed. After I have built up that idea, I tell the group, "But don't you worry, this is going to be a good talk." Since nobody has ever heard a speaker tell an audience at the start that his talk is going to be good, the group gets a great kick out of this.

They feel that I am a regular fellow, one they would like to know.

Another plan I use is to kid the officers about the way they have needled me into getting set to make a good talk. I explain how all sales executive clubs needle the speaker to make him give a good talk. I tell what happened in a number of towns. Then I wind up with something that happened here just tonight. This kidding of the local officers is good; the members themselves do it, and they feel that a man who does the same thing is one of them. That's one of your problems—to make yourself one of them.

Many times the other speakers give you a lead that will help you get started. Not long ago I appeared on a program where the other speaker was a man named Kelly. I made a crack about this being Irish night. Kelly liked it, and the audience did too. You might pick out a remark that a preceding speaker made and say something about that. Such remarks tell the audience that you are one of them . . . that you were there and perhaps suffering through the other speeches too.

In these references to other speakers try to be complimentary. It might be well to warn the other speaker that you are going to mention him, tell him what you will say, and ask if he has any objection. He will tell you if he has, or perhaps his manner will suggest that you skip the whole thing.

I find, too, that I can tee off on the introduction I am given, especially if the chairman uses the piece I have written. I start by saying that the introduction was good. I thank the chairman for what he said. I compliment him on the way he said it. I sometimes ask the audience to give the chairman a hand for it. After the applause, I explain that it should be good and accurate because I wrote it.

At times the introduction will be unbelievably mixed up. Once I spoke at a meeting where the chairman was depending on written descriptions of the speakers in the association magazine. When he started to introduce me, he couldn't find the blurb about me in the magazine. Here's about what he said:

"Our next speaker comes from the Westinghouse Company. Westinghouse is a big company and I don't know just which part of the Westinghouse Company this speaker comes from. He must be a good speaker, for I don't think the Westinghouse Company is in the habit of sending out speakers who can't do a good job of representing them. I don't know exactly what his subject is but it has something to do with training. I give you Mr. Hegarty of the Westinghouse Company."

All the chairman knew was my name and the name of my company. I used this inept introduction to tee off as follows:

"I'm glad your chairman introduced me that way. In fact I asked him to do it. You know why I did that? It gives me a chance to tell you what business I'm in. I'm in the part of the Westinghouse Company that has something to sell to you—electric refrigerators, electric ranges, Laundromats, that automatic washing machine that takes all the work out of washing, the electric clothes drier that probably saves more labor than any other appliance ever made, electric irons, toasters, waffle irons, roasters, and other appliances. They are all good value; they save time, work, and money." By now the audience was smiling. "That's a commercial," I went on. "Since I'm talking for free, the chairman agreed that I could use it."

The listeners like that type of thing. They figure that Hegarty is a regular guy. The chairman gave him a bad introduction, but he covered for the chairman and made everything seem regular.

Since the chairman was one of them, I might have appeared to be a sorehead if I had taken offense at such an introduction, and I had slight grounds, for I had traveled over 1,200 miles at my company's expense to make the talk. When I made capital out of it, the listeners figured that I was a regular fellow who took such slights good naturedly, in stride, and laughed them off.

In any of these stunts I make sure that I do not say anything that might reflect on the officers of the club. If you kid them, boost them too. Boosting always pays. That is true even if you don't get paid for speaking. Any such kidding should be in a friendly, complimentary vein.

Note that I said I wrote out what I wanted the chairman to say about me. Since I speak a lot, I have this on a mimeographed form.

If you write out what you want them to say, you have a better chance of getting the right kind of introduction. Even though you have mailed one of these introductions to the chairman, I suggest you carry an extra copy with you. Clubs have a habit of losing material or of sending it to the member who can't be at the meeting that night. With the extra copy you are prepared for anything. You are ready when a fellow rushes up to you and says, "Joe Whosis, who was to introduce you, can't be here tonight and I'm to do the honors. Do you have anything you want me to say about you?" Always give that fellow your prepared piece. You can't let him go ahead on his own. I have tried that and have been introduced as the boss of my boss—who happened to be sitting in the audience. That could prove embarrassing. The written introduction can help you get off to a good start.

If you are speaking on a technical subject, that written description of you and what you have done can help make the audience feel you are competent to talk on the subject. If you happen to look young for the subject and it appears that you have not been around long enough to get the experience needed, you might ask the chairman to be sure to read that part of the description.

When you are talking on a technical subject to a popular audience, you should establish early in your speech the reason why it should interest them. They sit there asking, "What does it mean to me?" Tell them quickly. I don't think you can do it in a sentence; it may take two or three. But be sure to tie it in with their experiences and interests.

Now, how can you explain how you know something about your subject? I heard a young engineer establish his competence with this statement: "You may wonder why I should be talking on this subject today. Well, gentlemen, my company is a rather conservative company; yet in the last three years the management has allowed me to spend about three hundred thousand dollars experimenting with this phenomenon. With that much experimenting I had to learn something, enough to write five semiannual reports, anyway."

I happened to know that this young man was the top expert in the country on his subject. But see how modestly he handled a description of his competence.

This is important. You don't want to give the impression that you are a know-it-all. And you don't want to indicate that you are better than the listeners in any way. You have seen speakers make this mistake. I imagine, though, that they didn't know what they were doing and would have been most surprised to learn that they were high-hatting the audience. If the audience doesn't know you, it is always suspicious of you. They're asking themselves, "Who's this guy anyway, and where does he get off, trying to tell us anything?"

You can open by complimenting the group on something. One of my friends starts his talk with, "When I was asked to speak on this subject to this *highly intelligent* group." He pauses on those words in italics. The opening always gets a smile; the audience likes it. You have heard speakers compliment the audience on something about their fair city, about their dress, about the hall, or the number present.

Clubs like this kind of thing. The members like to feel that the club is alive and is doing good for the community. The compliment is good, but you should be sure you are complimenting the group on the right thing. One of my friends complimented a club on a civic project that a city had just completed. It happened that the club had fought this project. When using the compliment, don't lay it on too thick. In any talk, insincerity shows through.

Another good starting device is to cut yourself down to the size of the group—a few steps under it is better. Not long ago I heard a speaker start, "As I look at you people tonight, I feel a little out of place. I come from out in California, and in my country the men who attend meetings like this come in sport shirts and they don't wear neckties. Now all you men are wearing neckties. You know, I don't know whether or not I'm good enough to talk to a group of men with neckties."

I worked in New York City for years, and time and again I heard a speaker from out of town start by mentioning the fact that he was just a country boy and didn't know how his talk would go in the big city.

I heard another speaker start thus: "I don't know why they picked me to make this talk. I'm no public speaker. Of course, I've been working with the stuff for years. I guess I could answer almost all the questions on it. But I am warning you now—this isn't going to be an oration." Note what this fellow did. He established the fact that he was an expert on the subject even though he admitted that he was not much of a speaker. With this kind of start you have to be careful not to depreciate too much. You have to remember that when you are before an audience you are supposed to be an expert.

Another way of warming up that cold audience is to ask them to get into the act . . . to do something for you. This may be a show of hands. A show of hands is a simple request. I do one which is most effective with large or small audiences. I ask the group to say "Hello" to me. I tell them that in my schools for salesmen I have the men greet me every morning with, "Good morning, Ed Hegarty." I ask if they think they can do that. I say, "Good morning, everybody." They reply, "Good morning, Ed Hegarty." This stunt has become pretty much of a trade-mark wherever I go. But the audience loves it. Of course I am never satisfied with the way they do it the first time; I want it louder, with more enthusiasm. Thus we do it three times and by then the audience is with me.

This can be carried further in large groups where the group members may not know the man in the next seat. You can have the men sitting next to one another shake hands and introduce themselves. This always loosens up a group. Many times the audience will seem slow in responding to one of these requests. That's because they don't expect the request. They have listened to the chairman's introduction and they have settled down in their seats. They are willing to let you do the work. In fact, the expression on many of the faces dares you to interest them. Thus your request throws them; it isn't routine. You have to convince them that you really mean it. Then you have to work to get them to do what you want. This effort helps you get over your initial nervousness and the stunt gets the group with you.

Now, analyze these suggestions for getting started. Some of them are quite simple, aren't they? Well, for that next speech why not try the one that seems easiest for you? You want to get started right, you want this group to think favorably of you—then why not give yourself a flying start by trying these things:

1. Put on your biggest de luxe smile. Beam at them. Pause; give it time to sink in.
2. Stand up straight, your chest out, your hands in front of you, not on the lectern.
3. Radiate enthusiasm for this job and this subject.
4. Talk louder than you think necessary. A bit louder than the chairman.
5. Try to convince the audience that you are a regular fellow by some good-natured kidding of the chairman, the committee, the officers, or the introduction which you wrote. Such kidding should be complimentary.
6. Establish the fact that you are competent to talk on the subject without being high-hat about it.
7. If they don't understand what the subject means to them, tell them early.
8. Compliment the group on something if you can do it sincerely.
9. Cut yourself down to the size of the group, but don't depreciate your abilities or subject.
10. Give the group a chance to get into the act.

That's all you need to know about the opening of your speech. Next comes the use of some of the speech elements mentioned on page 13. Remember them—the anecdote, news, and that language of yours. How about starting with the anecdote?

5

Using the Anecdote

There are few great speakers who aren't good at telling stories. If you check the experienced speaker, you will be surprised at the number of times he resorts to the story form. If you are going to become a good speaker, you should learn all you can about how the story can be used.

In the start of my talk "How to Get Better," I kid the title a bit. And how do I do it? With a story, of course. Now with that intriguing title a man might talk about anything. Since I happen to use charts with this talk, the listeners are looking at a chart reading "How to Get Better," and I know that they are asking, "How to get better what?"

Now I could start by saying, "As I look at your faces this evening with all your eyes on this chart, I know what you are asking. You are asking, 'How to get better what?' "

There is nothing wrong with that kind of start, but I point that question up a bit by putting it in story form.

Here is my wording: "The other night when I was leaving the office the publicity man said, 'I hear you are going to make a speech in Pittsburgh.'

" 'That's right,' I said.

" 'What are you going to talk about?' he asked.

" 'My subject is "How to Get Better." '

"And do you know what he asked me? He asked, 'How to get better what?' "

By putting the idea in a story I get a smile, sometimes a laugh, and I have pointed up the subject.

A story about the invitation to talk, a story about why they picked you, a story about the subject—where you got it, why it is good, why it is timely, why you feel so strongly about it—all these are good.

There is not much point to the story above. All it does is emphasize my title. Note that in the story the title is mentioned twice. I get repetition, and that is about all. Let's say I wanted to play up the importance of the subject. In my story, then, I have the publicity man, or anyone else, ask, "Why should you be wasting the time of an audience on a subject like that?"

Such a question gives me an excellent lead for a story on why it is important that anyone get better. If it was a subject that I had to justify, I could build up the story by asking various friends or associates how they felt about it. Your story can be as short as the one I used or it can be as long as you want to make it.

How do you tell such stories? Well, the first requirement of a serious story is that it must be believed. Don't report an incident that couldn't have happened. When you tell such a story, even though you have made it up, try to think of a friend as the other fellow in the story. Think of him as you tell it. When you speak the story as if you are seeing Joe, your pal, right there before you, you can make the story seem much more plausible.

Such stories fall into a few patterns.

You talk to somebody.

You tell of something you saw or did.

You explain how somebody showed something to you.

You report on an experience.

You put a quotation in story form.

The story about the "How to Get Better" title shows how a story can be built by talking to somebody. Most of the stories I tell in my sales talks come from my conversations with others. Let's say you are a captain of the Community Chest drive. You read in the literature or in the campaign material that the worker who will make ten calls on homes will get five subscriptions. Next week when you get your team together you want to use that figure . . . you want them to make those calls and get those subscriptions. Now you can prepare a grand talk on that material in the campaign brochure, but think how much better your talk would go over if you went out and made ten calls and then told the story of what happened. You have live material. The story of your experiences would be far more effective than anything else.

Let's say you want your story to prove a point. One good way to do this is to introduce the story with the statement of what you are trying to prove. You state your premise. You tell your story to prove the premise, and then you wind up with a restatement of your premise.

Let's say your premise is that if a worker makes ten calls on this fund drive he will get five subscriptions. Here is an example of how you might handle it.

"This piece of campaign literature I have here in my hand is called 'Instructions to Workers.' It says this—here, I'll read it to you." (Read from piece.) "If you will make ten calls each night, you will get five subscriptions. I wonder how many of you believe that. The night before last I didn't, and early last night I didn't. But tonight I believe it; and do you know why? Because, last night I went out and made ten calls. And what did I find out? Let me tell you."

Now you go into the story of how you went out and made the ten calls and got not five subscriptions but six. Report on one call, two, or all ten. Admit that maybe you were lucky in beating the average. But you made the average, and that was what you were trying to prove.

When you finish your story, wind up with a statement like this: "I said I didn't believe that statement, that five out of ten stuff. But tonight I do believe. Why? Because I went out and found out that it was true. And if a poor salesman like me—I think I'm the world's worst—can better that average, think what you can do."

The form of this story is good because it proves that you were wrong. In telling this kind of story don't make it appear that you know the answers. Audiences would rather listen to a speaker who can be wrong. That line, "I'm the world's worst," is good for any story you tell. It indicates that you are not a know-it-all.

The anecdote that explains how somebody showed something to you is used a lot in product talks. Let's say you want to explain the fine qualities of a common wooden pencil. You talk about the yellow enamel that is baked on, about the brass on the end that holds the eraser, how it is clinched to the wood, the lead, how it is large and soft and makes a black mark, and the eraser on the end, how it is soft and erases the black mark with a light pressure.

Now that doesn't sound like an exciting story, does it? And it isn't exciting, except to a man or woman who sells pencils. Well, let's say you sell pencils and you want to make your story interesting. Could you do it with a story, like this?

"I have here in my hand a common yellow pencil. But the other day in a store on Main Street, I met a young lady behind a counter who told me this about that pencil. . . ." Now you go into the description. Will your story have more interest? It surely will.

If you have a quotation that helps prove your point, you can use a story to point it up. I heard a speaker do that recently. He wanted to quote Gen. Dwight Eisenhower, and he told how he had met the General at a party and had asked him a question. His quote got more attention because he chose to build a story around it.

When you are talking about a product, plan, or procedure you can break up the description by such stories. The story gives your point more life, and it varies the monotony of straight description.

Where do you get the material for such stories? Well, you have to listen and you have to ask questions. As you meet the chairman of the meeting at which you are to talk, he will no doubt make a remark that might be used in such a story. If I am looking for such material before a talk, I usually get what I am after by asking a few questions.

As I travel about the country, I overhear remarks that might be used. Here are three that I picked up recently. I heard all of them in restaurants:

Two friends met unexpectedly and one said, "Paul, you old son of a gun, what a pleasure." Now that might be the basis of a story that illustrated how a man can go all out to let the other know he is glad to see him.

When another two men met, one of them asked, "Still married to the same woman?" That might be used in an illustration of what not to say to make friends.

Out of another group talking I heard this remark, "The guy's got no handle on him." I talk a lot about getting along with people and that remark will come in handy, I know.

The experiences you have as you travel about will give you material for stories. Not long ago I checked into a hotel. As the bellman took me upstairs, two other men stepped into the elevator. The bellman greeted one of them, "Good evening, Mr. Travis."

"Hello, there," said Mr. Travis. Mr. Travis had a newspaper in his hand, and as we started, he said, "I don't know why I bought this newspaper; I've lost my glasses."

"Would you like to try mine?" the bellman said. He took a pair out of his pocket and handed them to the gentleman. "Go on, try them," he said. "I never use them."

Mr. Travis put on the glasses. He said, "Yeah, I can read with these."

"Keep them, then," the bellman said. "You can return them when you get a new pair of your own. I never use them. I just happened to find them in my locker this morning."

Travis thanked him and got off.

Now that can be used as the story of a man who gave extra service. The bellman knew that hotel guests were misplacing or losing their glasses; so he carried a pair around to help them out.

I tell the story just as it happened. Then I say, "As we walked down to my room on one of the higher floors, I asked the bellman, 'Say, what is the idea of these glasses?'

" 'Oh, that,' he laughed. 'I got three pair of them.'

" 'But how did you know this fellow could see through them?'

" 'Anybody can see through them. They're dime-store glasses. All they do is magnify.'

" 'You get many guests who lose their glasses?'

" 'Mister, you'd be surprised. I'll bet that pair of specs back there has paid me ten bucks in tips already this year.' "

You can see that the story would make good speech material. I got it because I kept my ears open and asked a few questions. When you see something or hear something that looks as if it might make a speech story, ask some questions and fill in the details.

Anecdotes in which you figure are better speech material than stories about things that happen to the neighbors. In telling tales, put yourself into the action. Even if the owl did get down the neighbor's chimney, have it perching on the chandelier in your living room when you tell the story in a speech. The story is better when you get into the action as deeply as you can. You might start, "I read in the newspaper this morning. . . ." Such a statement puts you into the story, but you are not too deeply involved. When you say, "A fellow telephoned me this morning and told me . . ." or "I met a man on the street this morning . . . ," you are more a part of the action. But it is better to get in all the way, say that you saw it, you were there, it happened to you.

You may say, "But in this story I want to use, I wasn't there. It happened to a friend of mine." That is all right; couldn't it have happened to you? If this story has a restaurant for its setting, couldn't you have been in the restaurant instead of the friend? These listeners can picture you; they may not be able to picture your friend.

In putting yourself into stories, don't overdo. Don't put yourself into a situation that is obviously incredible. The impossible might be all right—"Last night I died and went to Heaven"—but not the incredible. Stay clear of situations they won't believe. The locale you use should seem natural to you. If you want to put yourself into a story about Southern mountaineers, explain that last summer, when you were traveling in Tennessee, you met some mountain people, and so on and so forth. After the meeting a listener will be sure to ask you what part of the state you were in.

You say, "Oh, about one hundred miles south of Nashville." With that as a clue he will tell you where you were.

But if there is to be a hero in your story, let it be your small son Johnny, or your wife, or the gardener. Don't pose as the hero in any of your tales. A story goes over better if you seem to get the worst of it. Remember, this audience is looking at you and it is not too difficult for them to picture you as slightly lacking in common horse sense. You are demanding too much when you ask them to picture you as a hero.

Try to vary the locale of the stories you tell. It is not good to have too many stories about hotels and bellmen, or about bars and grills and bartenders. Locate one in the office, one at home, one on the street, and another at the meeting of the Sons of the American Revolution.

As you study stories that are told in speeches, you find that most of them are built on a plan that allows three things to happen. A man talking about accidents in the home might say, "I have read that a high percentage of all accidents happen in the home. I didn't believe that until the other night when I saw how it could be true. I started down into my basement without turning on the light. On the stairs I tripped over my boy's overshoes. I caught myself but I might have fallen all the way down. Well, I was too far away from the upstairs light switch now, so I went on. Two steps, and I ran into a clothesline my wife had stretched. It caught me right under the nose—it might have caught me in the eye. I started into the next room and ran into the closed door. That's the first time I've known that door to be closed."

Note that there are three accidents. By bringing in the three you build up suspense. Had the speaker stopped with the tripping over the overshoes, he would not have had much of a story, would he? If he had stopped with running into the clothesline, he would have lost some of the suspense. But by the time he runs into the door he has gone about as far as he can go. His hearers can imagine him swearing mildly at that first mishap. By the time he hits the clothesline he has begun a slow burn. Then when he runs into that door he is ready to explode.

When you build a story for your next speech, think of this grouping in threes. If you have a story you tell now that goes over well, see if you can revise it to fit into this "one, two, three" plan. Try the revised version, and see if it won't go better.

Sometimes you have felt that the speaker memorized every word of his stories and was trying to remember the words rather than trying to tell you a story. I suggest you learn your stories, not the words. Tell the story in your own words. When you lift a story about a famous character out of a book, you are inclined to use some of the writer's language in telling your story. Try to avoid words that don't speak well. You will sound much more natural if you do.

Forget the formal type of introduction when you tell a story. Recently I heard a speaker say, "I would like to relate a little incident that happened to me. . . ." Such an introduction doesn't sound as if it belongs to you. Neither does one like "They tell a story about Lincoln. . . ." or "It is well illustrated by a story they tell about Lincoln. . . ." Start your story with a line like "The other day . . ." or "Last week in Cleveland. . . ." Lines of that kind sound natural. Listen to the introductions most speakers use for stories and you find that the introduction is not needed.

A story goes better when the group feels that you are speaking extemporaneously. You may memorize and rehearse each story, but try to give the impression that you are unrehearsed. You might do that in a number of ways:

You might pause. The thing that usually tips off the fact that the piece is memorized is that the speaker tends to go on faster and faster as he continues with the memorized piece.

You might throw in an aside. This has the same effect as a pause. It indicates that you are telling a story just as you might tell it across the luncheon table. The aside is something you just happened to think of.

Keep your eyes on the audience. Don't glance at the ceiling light as if you were trying to think of the exact word, or as if you were trying to think of your point.

Try to loosen up as you start the story; work in a movement

of your arms or your hands. Any such movement tends to relax you. The fellow who has memorized a speech usually seems stiff and rigid trying to think of the words he has to remember.

You can move, take a few steps to the right or left if you are not anchored by a lectern. Shift your weight from one foot to the other, now stand at attention, now parade rest; such movement tends to make you seem relaxed.

A smile is a big help in hiding the fact that you have memorized the wording. The fellow who has memorized always has a worried look as if trying to remember what word comes next.

Your own words will help in this. If you memorize a word you do not use regularly or a word that is difficult for you to pronounce, you may tip off the fact that you memorized. Use simple words in your stories. If the story has difficult words, change them to ones you might use in conversation.

In many of your stories you will want to memorize sentences. You will surely want to memorize the line that makes the point; most speakers do. But rehearse the lines so that you sound rather casual when you say them. This happened to you, and this is how it was. If the audiences sense that you have memorized the script and are worrying about words, they are less likely to believe.

Use "I said," "he said," and "she said" in explaining most of your remarks. Don't describe how he said it by such expressions as "with exasperation" or "with fire in his eye." Those are literary descriptions, good in type but not so good when spoken.

When you quote a character, the language must seem natural. If your character is a truck driver, have him speak in the language of a truck driver. Don't have him say, "For goodness' sake." He would probably use a stronger expression.

Try to vary your voice when the other fellow speaks to you. Speak your lines in your own voice and the other fellow's in a different tone. You might have the other fellow speak a little faster or slower than you do. You might also try turning your head a bit to one side when one speaks, slightly to the other side when the other speaks. Your hands, your shoulders, and your facial expressions can help when you tell stories. You might practice telling the stories in front of a mirror to see how far you can go with expressions or with the movement of your head. In this way you dramatize your stories.

Most speakers try to shorten their stories too much. You have to give the audience a chance to realize that you are started on the telling of a story before you finish. They want to hear your story; they want to enjoy it. Many times the story you have is too thin. You need to build it up . . . to lengthen it. Usually you can do that by having one of the characters in the story ask a question of you, or you can ask a question of the character. One additional question and answer might give the story all the body it needs. You want the story to help you make your point. If it finishes too fast, the group may not get the idea. Study your stories to see if they get over. If the audience does not seem to get the point, try adding a question and answer. It may help get the effect you want.

If you want to learn to speak well in public, learn all you can about telling stories. Practice using the anecdote in conversation. Become expert at illustrating points with stories—not the so-called funny story, but the anecdote that helps you make your point. It is the speaker's best friend.

Here is a summation of these suggestions:

1. Use an anecdote to point up your subject.
2. Use only stories that are not too difficult to believe.
3. Try to keep before you a picture of the characters that appear in the story.
4. Make sure your story helps prove your point.
5. Instead of making a statement, tell a story that illustrates that statement.
6. Put yourself in all your stories but never make yourself the hero.
7. Vary the locale of your stories.
8. Study the law of "one, two, three." Make three things happen in a story.
9. Vary the voice to indicate the characters, if you can.
10. Try to vary your voice when the other fellow speaks to you in a story.

11. Use a natural introduction to your stories, not "This point is illustrated by a story about Pat and Mike." Go directly into the story.
12. Use "he said" and "she said" in explaining the remarks. Eliminate most explanations of how the remarks were made.
13. When you quote a character, use words the character might use.
14. Study the stories you use. Do they help you hold interest? Do they help make the points? If not, improve or discard them.
15. Don't let your stories finish so fast that the audience will miss the point.

6

How to Get the Laughs

Every speaker seems to want to get laughs. He wants the listeners to laugh at his quips, his imitations. He needs those laughs, for they are a tonic, they lift him up, they encourage him to do better. But they can fool him, too, for they may overshadow the points he wants to make in his speech.

You may say, "Not me, I have trouble getting any laughs."

When a man tells me that, I ask, "Have you ever studied how other speakers get laughs?"

"Sure I have," he replies. "They tell stories and get laughs. I tell the same stories and get nothing."

"Do you have any idea of what they did that you didn't do?"

"No, I think I tell the story just as they did."

He thinks he did, and perhaps he did. But probably he didn't do it just right. It is much like baking a cake. One woman bakes a beauty and gives the recipe to another. The second follows the recipe and her cake falls flat. What made the difference? "I did everything just as it said," the woman protests. Yet the second cake was not right. Perhaps it is knack, or experience, or tricks of the trade.

I like to think that tricks get laughs; so let's discuss a few tricks that speakers use to get them. There are scores of forms of humor used in talks. Here is a list of the forms that are most popular with speakers:

Funny story
Wisecrack

Pun
Simile
Definition or daffynition
Aside
Humorous poem

That is a shortened list, but it covers most of the forms you might use. So let's talk about each form.

But let's get this straight at the start. You don't have to be funny if you don't want to. There is no law. From listening to speakers you might get the idea that every speaker must have a fund of funny stories on which he can draw at will. Most good speakers are so equipped. And most of them are good at storytelling.

I have a friend who starts each speech with a number of stories. He tells story after story until he has the crowd in stitches. Once I asked him, "Why do you tell all those gag stories at the start of your speeches?"

"There is method in it, Ed," he replied. "I loosen up the audience with those stories. When they are loose, I go to work on them."

My friend's "story, story, story" gets his audience into the mood. One of the reasons why a story may not get a laugh is that the audience is not in the mood for a laugh. As you stand up to speak and look out over those doubtful, questioning faces, you feel just a bit discouraged. When you have a cold audience, you have to work harder; you have to throw more energy into what you say and do. My friend's plan of loosening them up with his stories can be classed as a warm-up. Radio programs with studio audiences do this. The comedian cracks a few jokes and gets the audience in the mood to laugh and applaud before the program goes on the air.

Another friend always starts his speech with a funny story, usually one he has heard recently. He is not a gifted storyteller, and his stories usually fall flat. One night I asked him, "You know you can't tell stories. Why do you always start your speeches with a story?"

"I tell it for its effect on me," he said. "It seems to get me over that initial nervousness."

Both of these men have reasons for telling their stories. One is good at it; the other isn't. Yet both are using the story to do a job for them. And that is the way you should use the funny story in a speech—as something with a purpose. Perhaps there is a spot in the speech that needs a lift. You feel you must have a funny story at that point. O.K., tell your story and tie it in as closely as you can with the point you want to make. Usually it does not take too much imagination to use the gag line in the story to further your point. So when the laugh has subsided, speak the line that ties the story into the fabric of your speech.

If you are going to use the funny story, you have to condition yourself. You have to enjoy telling funny stories. But further, you have to show the audience that you enjoy them—by your mood, your manner, your enthusiasm. When you start a story, try to give the impression that "this is going to be good."

One good device for putting yourself into a story is dialect. When you use dialect, you force yourself to get into the story. You may say, "I can't handle dialect stories." You may be right; very few speakers can. But they try, and after some practice they don't do too poorly. You might start by learning one dialect, say Irish. You need only a few words. Pick out a character on the radio or television, and see how good an imitation you can do. If you can get yourself into your stories and let yourself go, you will make a hit with the stories you tell.

Start your story fast. Don't use an elaborate introduction that takes something from the story. Sneak up on the audience with that story; make it so much a part of the speech that they don't realize you are into a story until you have them riding with you.

You also want to arouse expectancy and anticipation. You want to build up the suspense. In the last few weeks I have heard speakers use these lines to help build up suspense:

"I guess I can tell it here."

"The boss doesn't like me to tell this story on him, so if you hear I'm fired you'll know why."

"While this is secret stuff, I don't think we have any men who should not know it."

"Any Democrats in the room?"

As you look at those remarks, you can see how the speaker was trying to build up suspense with them. All were a part of anecdotes. Some speakers like to build up the listeners' expectancy with such remarks as:

"Wait until you hear this."

"Boy, this is good."

Description and dramatization of the characters in a story also help build up anticipation. I have a story I tell about an Indian selling an herb medicine. I believe it is one of the best stories I tell. Audience reaction seems to confirm this. In telling this story I describe how an Indian is dressed and painted. I imitate his voice. Those devices help build up anticipation. Whenever you can use a drawl or mimicry in imitating one of your characters, you add interest.

If you have noticed, most good storytellers take longer than the poor ones. They put in many colorful details. They prepare the listener, just as that warm-up on the radio program does.

Be sure to select only those stories that you think are funny. But you should be prepared for a surprise when you tell them. Many times the story that you thought was funny, that brought a laugh when you told it at the luncheon table, falls flat when you tell it to a group, even to an audience that is warmed up. I can't explain why, but it sometimes happens.

When the story falls flat, you can let it lie or you can do what the comedians on the radio do. You can comment on the flop. You can ask, "That wasn't a very good story, was it?" Sometimes that line will get the laugh you missed. You can say, "I'll have to get me some new writers." That may get the response. Not long ago I heard a speaker in this spot ask, "I wonder why that story isn't funny?" The audience pondered that thought, looked at him, and laughed.

At times, when this has happened to me, I have repeated the gag line. Here's how I do it. I tell my story. They sit there looking at me, nobody laughing. Then I repeat, "That was no lady, that was my wife." Now they realize that they were supposed to laugh, and they do. Repeating the gag line may also help button down the point. In such a situation you could paraphrase the Senator Claghorn line, "That's a joke, son." I have used a statement such as, "I didn't think that story was very funny, but I didn't know how bad it was until now."

It may be that the form of the story is what bothered the audience. In a gag story you have to give the group a chance to understand what you are up to. The story you pick out of the jokebook may be entirely too short for speaking. For that reason the wisecrack sometimes falls flat. You say, "A comma is a mark of punctuality." That talks mighty fast, doesn't it? Let's assume that line is funny and you want to use it in a speech. Why not make a story out of it?

You might say, "A teacher asked little Johnny, 'What is a comma?'

"Johnny said, 'I don't know.'

"She asked little Willy, 'Willy, can you tell me?'

"Willy shook his head. 'I don't know, teacher.'

"At this point little Tony held up his hand. 'Can you tell us, Tony?' asked the teacher.

" 'Yes, teacher,' Tony said.

" 'All right, Tony, you stand up, and I want all the rest of you to listen while Tony tells us. Stand up, Tony.'

"Tony stood up.

" 'All right, Tony, tell us.'

"Tony's face beamed. He said, 'A comma is a mark of punctuality.' "

Perhaps that was not a good gag to begin with. But it illustrates how the gag line should be built up for use in a speech. You have to give the audience an opportunity to get into the story. Your story should have four things:

1. Life. This gag line alone had little life. When the teacher and the kids were brought into it, it had life.

2. Suspense. You have to keep the audience wondering what is going to happen: one boy, a second boy, and then Tony.
3. It must keep moving. The teacher goes from one to the other searching for her answer.
4. A good gag line. In this case there may not be too much of a gag to start with, but the better your gag line, the better your laugh.

At this point you may say, "Look, Hegarty, I have heard a lot of speakers use gags like the one you mention, and they got laugh after laugh with them, too." That is right, you did, but the key to those laughs is the last part of your statement, "laugh after laugh." Remember the story earlier in this chapter of the man who tells story after story? After you once get an audience laughing, they expect you to make them laugh. If you study the speakers who use this "daffynition" technique, you will usually find that they started the audience laughing early. Then when they threw out a wisecrack, the audience continued laughing.

One difficulty with the wisecrack technique is that it is not as easy to tie the wisecrack to the subject as it is the gag line of a story. Many times you hear comments on talks that go, "He sure kept us laughing, but he didn't tell us much." You also hear, "He made no attempt to tie down his points." When you tell a joke, you want to tie it into your subject. Remember, the speaker's main purpose is to get the point over. The laughs are his compensation to the audience for sitting still and listening while he makes his point.

The pun is another form that may go too fast for the audience. Let's say you fancy this line: "A comedian is a man with hair on his jest." In speaking that line you may kill it for the audience by the speed with which you say it. Of course, the pun has another disadvantage. Remember how your associates act when you repeat a pun? Someone usually simulates a sudden illness. Use puns if you are good at it, or mix them with wisecracks. But prepare the audience for them. Make sure they will laugh at your longer stories before you try to get laughs with your quickies.

This advice on puns also goes also for those amusing similes, definitions, epigrams, bawled-up proverbs, moron stories, and the "Confucius say" sort of thing. They are funny, but usually they are too short and fast. You have heard that the hand is faster than the eye, but it is also true that sometimes the voice is faster than the ear. When you use these short forms, use them only after you have the audience warmed up.

Another liability, so far as speed is concerned, is that the pun is based on a play on words. Perhaps the touch is so fine that only those listening intently will get it. You can no doubt think of times when you had to read a wisecrack a second time to get it. Now a speaker can't repeat his gag line every time and ask, "Get it?" Watch, then, for the sledge-hammer type of gag if you use the quickie. Lay off the subtle one that needs deft handling.

Usually a speaker is trying to cut his material and he may feel that a little of this fast humor goes a long way. Use too little of it, and you may find that you don't do too well. Next time you hear a speaker use this kind of humor, check to see if he doesn't use lots of quickies. As you analyze, you may think he has too many. But he has found from experience how many he needs.

The humorous poem is another device you might use to get laughs. If you want to do a long poem, you have to memorize and rehearse it. Short poems such as you find in magazines make good material. Some speakers are good at reading this poetry. They can get laughs with it, too. Here's one of the kind I mean, picked from Josh Billings:

I hate to be a kicker,
I always long for peace,
But the wheel that squeaks the loudest
Is the one that gets the grease.

There is truth in that statement, and a bit of humor, too. You might get a laugh with it. And if you are trying to make the point that your audience should speak up about something or write to their congressmen, you have a light poem that you can use.

Many times you want to get that audience squeaking like the wheel that needs lubrication.

If you use a jingle, watch its length. The short poem may be too fast for the audience. Take this one:

If you get a valentine,
Signed "with love and kisses,"
Beware, my son! Some miss is
Set to be a Mrs.

It was written by A. S. Flaumenshaft, and appeared in *Pathfinder*. It is good, isn't it, when you read it? But try saying it. It goes fast, and that combination of s's may cause your audience to lose the last line. The shortness bothers me because the audience must listen to a poem long enough to understand what you are up to. They have to realize that you are reciting poetry. In a short bit like this, they may not catch up with what you are doing before you are on to the next idea. One way to overcome this is to announce that you are about to read a poem. Then take a card from your pocket and read slowly.

You hear many speakers make excellent use of the aside in their stories. They are going along with the story and they introduce a side thought. In my story about an Indian selling an herb medicine, I have this aside: "Oh, by the way, I'd better tell you this—I hadn't been listening to this Indian very long before I began to doubt that he was a real Indian. You know what tipped me off? This fellow had a habit of punctuating every paragraph with this question, 'Get the pernt?' " This explanation gets a laugh. But it is, of course, not the big laugh.

Now why do I use the aside? Well, I find that such a detour helps to build up suspense. In a story I tell about a bellhop, I say, "By the way, this boy I am telling you about was just about two years older than I am." Again the device gets a laugh, but its main purpose is to build up suspense. Watch the experienced storytellers to see how they use asides. And try to judge just how much the asides help in the telling of the story.

You also help build suspense by using the "one, two, three" incident technique explained in Chap. 5. You might have a good story with one incident, or with two, but usually you will do better with three. Examine your favorite story, and see if it follows this rule. If not, try revising it to put in three incidents. Of course, all stories are not built on this pattern, but most of the stories that consist of what-I-said-to-him and what-he-said-to-me can be built up that way. The "one, two, three" plan helps build suspense.

Let me repeat the advice given in Chap. 4 about using spoken words. You can't use the wording in those jokebooks; you have to change the words to spoken words before you use them. If you use spoken words, you can memorize your stories without the audience being aware that you speak from memory. Next time you think a speaker's talk is memorized, watch his wording. What makes you suspect that he memorized the script? Isn't it the way he handles some of the words? If you have to memorize a script, make sure that all the words are spoken words. Make sure, too, that they are words with which you are familiar and which you can pronounce.

Put yourself into your funny stories just as you do in the anecdotes. If the story is about a fellow going into a restaurant and talking to a waiter, change it so that you go into the restaurant and talk to the waiter. One man told me, "Ed, but that makes me ridiculous." What's wrong with that? Maybe it is not pleasing to your ego, but the audience will love it.

Here is a point to remember about stories. The audience likes stories in which you are the goat. They don't like stories in which you are the hero. If you try to make yourself the big guy in the story, the listeners feel that you are a show-off. When you put yourself in a story, remember that the audience is sitting there looking at you. Perhaps you don't look like a fellow who would be in the locale or the situation called for by the funny story. When I tell a story about stopping to watch a street peddler sell his wares, I explain why I do it. I say, "I am a student of selling. And who is the best salesman you can watch? Isn't it the man who works on the street? He has to be good enough to stop you while you are on your way somewhere. You salesmen in stores have the customers come to you. But not this street fakir; he has to be good enough to stop you and hold you with his story and his demonstration. And so I always stop to watch and listen to such fakirs. I learn a lot from them."

Now that I have explained my reason for stopping, I can go on with my story without the man in the audience doubting that I would stop. Such an explanation helps make the story plausible to the group.

Putting yourself in the story rules out many funny stories for you. On the other hand, you might not see how you can put yourself into a story of a man who dies and goes up to the gates of Heaven, but I heard a speaker do just that not so long ago. He said, "I dreamed that I had died and gone up to the gates of Heaven." Now he was all set to meet Saint Peter, and the audience could picture him throwing his hat over the gate and saying, "You'll have to let me get in to get my hat." Of course, such a line would violate the rule that you are to be the goat instead of the hero, but there are exceptions to all rules.

I would advise against telling the vulgar or risqué story in public. It is mighty easy to build up a reputation for telling stories of that kind. Surely the stag audience laughs at such stories. But you have to ask yourself, "Am I that kind of a guy?" To get a picture of the kind of guy you mean, think of a friend or acquaintance who tells such stories. How do you feel about him? I stay clear of such stories. Usually you can find a clean story that is funny and that gets just as much applause. In your talk you represent something—a company, a cause, a plan—and—most important—yourself.

I would advise you also to lay off racial or religious stories. They may offend someone, and you are not there to do that. You have a plan or an idea to present and you want a favorable reaction from everybody. Why take a chance of offending even one of the group? The laugh is not worth that much. And remember, with a little work you can often change the story so that it offends nobody and still gets the laugh you want.

Now comes that most important part of your story—the gag line. The audience will listen all through the build-up, but if they don't get the gag line, they won't laugh. This was to be a funny story; you needed a laugh at this point in the speech—remember?

Well, they have to hear that line and they have to understand it. Then they have to know that the story is finished and that it is time to laugh. The group is sitting there in suspense, anticipating. They are trying to figure what your gag line is. You have tried to give them no hint of it. Perhaps you can tell from their faces that some of them have heard the story before. But that is not bad. Think how, when you are in an audience, you like to hear a speaker tell a story you have heard before; it gives you a feeling that you know something that the others don't know. Then think of the times when a speaker has started a story you have heard before, but you can't remember the gag line. Yes, even those people who have heard your story are waiting to enjoy the denouement. Then why not organize to do that gag line right?

Here are some suggestions: separate the gag line; see that it has no unusual words; watch your timing, not too fast; watch your pronunciation; speak the key words distinctly and a bit louder than the rest of the story.

The first suggestion is to separate it, get it off by itself. What do I mean by that? Let's illustrate with the story about the teacher and the kids. The gag line is, "A comma is a mark of punctuality." These words are the last line of the story. They are apart. There is no description of how Tony said them. Tony says his piece, and the story is finished. Thus we have the gag line separated.

Next the gag line should have no unusual words. In that pun example the line was, "A comedian is a man with hair on his jest." The word "jest" will not speak too well. Yet without the word you have no gag. But the line is one that will not be understood by many of the audience. Sure, they know what a jest is, but they won't hear the word. My suggestion on the gag line is that it should be in familiar words. Tony's line in the story rates well in this. All the words are familiar.

Timing is important in the gag line. Say it slowly. Give the words a chance to sink in. A lengthy gag line requires some study in timing. In my Indian story, the gag line is rather long. The Indian tells the audience that they don't know how to cook vegetables. They put the vegetables in a pan. They put the pan on top of the stove. They cover the vegetables with water. They boil the vegetables to beat the band, until they have cooked the vitamins out of them into the water. Then what do they do? They hold the lid in place on top of the pan, they walk over to the sink, and they pour the water with the vitamins in it down the drain. They'd be better off if they drank the water and threw the vegetables away. Now comes the gag line. The Indian says, "And what happens to them vitamins when they go down the sink? I'll tell you. They go down into the sewer. And the rats eat them. And they get strong. And you get weak."

Note that that gag line has been broken up into five sentences. Each is spoken slowly. As I come to the last sentences, I am speaking about as slowly as I can. The breaking down into sentences helps with the timing. I am trying to build up to those last eight words.

In speaking the last line, I raise my voice. I speak more slowly; I give it more volume. By putting more volume into my voice, I make sure that more of the audience will hear and there will be fewer of the brothers nudging neighbors and asking "What did he say?" If the gag line is to register, they have to hear it.

Make sure you speak the key words distinctly. Slowing up helps. Speaking louder helps, too. But even with the slowing up and extra volume, watch your pronunciation. Snap off those key words. I make a point to hit the words "strong" and "weak." I am careful of how I pronounce them. You may say, "Look, Hegarty, they're easy words—who could mess them up?" You'd be surprised. Maybe you couldn't, but it is a good idea to make sure you won't.

Recently, after I had finished a speech, one of my friends said, "Ed, you gave us a lesson in timing." He meant that I had done the things I have suggested here. Organize that gag line for speaking, speak it slowly, raise your voice when you say it, and pronounce the key words clearly.

In telling funny stories try to build up to the end. First comes the small incident, then one of more importance, and then the big one. As you talk, things get a bit worse with each new fact. Then when you come to the big thing, you have built up suspense. The audience is ready; they are anxious to hear how it came out. This is no time to lose them by mumbling words, talking too low, or going too fast. Remember, you know what happened. You are trying to tell them. So do it slowly. Take your time. You have wasted all the time you took to tell the story if you don't get over that gag line.

When you first take up the practice of telling stories, concentrate on learning how to handle the gag line. Master that and then learn how to start and how to build up suspense. Your pay-off is the gag line. You can tell the first part of your story like a novice, but you must tell the end of it like a professional. For it is that last part that gets the laugh.

Storytellers develop a faculty for what I call snapping the whip. They build up to the gag line so that it cracks like the end of a whip. In one of my talks on selling I use this story:

"Not long ago I went into a hardware store to buy some screws. I wanted extra-large screws and I told the salesman what I wanted. The fellow got the screws and counted out the eight I needed. Then he said, 'Do you have a screw driver to fit these screws?'

"Well, I'm like any other fellow with a house. I had four or five screw drivers, but here was a new idea. 'Sure, I've got a screw driver,' I said.

" 'I mean to fit these screws,' the salesman said. 'Here, I'll show you what I mean.' He went over to the case and took out a screw driver. He put the blade of the screw driver into the slot of the screw and he showed me. Then he said, 'Now, if the blade of the screw driver fits the slot exactly like this you won't tear the screw and you won't harm the screw driver.'

"He picked up another screw driver. 'Here,' he said, 'you see this screw driver is too small. If you try to drive this screw with this screw driver, you'll tear the screwhead and harm the screw driver.'

"Well, you know what happened? I bought a new sixty-five-cent screw driver that fitted that screw. I didn't know whether or not any screw driver I had at home would fit that screw. And I got out of that store fast. Why?

"Well, confidentially, I was afraid that he might try to sell me a file to sharpen the screw driver when the point got dull. If I was sucker enough to buy a file, he might sell me a file brush to clean the file. Why, if I hadn't run out of that store before that guy was through, I might have owned more hardware than he did."

Those last two lines get a laugh when I'm talking to salesmen from hardware stores. A good salesman might think of the screw driver to fit the screw. A supersalesman might think of a file to keep the screw-driver point in good shape, but it would take a genius to think of selling a device to clean the file after it has been used.

In my talk on "How to Run a Sales Meeting" one of my rules is "Don't Compete with Anything." In that talk I have a sequence like this.

"Whenever anyone comes into the room or anyone is called out, stop your speech and wait until the commotion ends. If the boss's secretary comes in to whisper something in the boss's ear, stop your talk until she is through whispering." I pause here; then say:

"They want to hear what she is saying to the boss anyway."

In that sequence the line, "They want to hear what she is saying to the boss," gets a laugh. It helps make the point but it gets a laugh, too.

In the same talk, in my sequence on charts in making another point, "Don't Use the Same Introduction to Each Chart," I tell this story:

"Not long ago I was in Canton, and a fellow running a meeting with a set of charts used the same introduction to each one. As he turned the chart, he would say, 'This chart is supposed to show. . . .' He'd talk awhile, and then turn to the next chart and say, 'This chart is supposed to show. . . .' He came to the third chart and again he said, 'This chart is supposed to show. . . .'

"By this time he had the audience doing it with him. When he reached down to pick up the bottom of the fourth chart to turn it over, the audience was mentally saying, 'This chart is supposed to show. . . .' "

Again it's that snapping of the whip, going from the sublime to the ridiculous.

At a meeting recently I heard a speaker talking about the notes he was taking. He said, "I sat there in that meeting taking notes. For one day, for two days, for three days, for four days. At the end of those four days I had enough notes to fill forty-eight typewritten pages. Why, that's enough copy to fill a newspaper, three magazines, and four sheets of Kleenex."

It's that last line, "four sheets of Kleenex," that got the laugh. He made his point, but he cracked the whip and got a laugh with it.

Elmer Wheeler, who does some expert talking on sales subjects, is a master at snapping the whip. Talking about the poor service you get in restaurants, he said, "Today you go into a restaurant and order buttered toast. After a wait the toast comes. It is not buttered. You push the toast a bit; you turn the plate to see if a microscopic bit of butter is hidden behind the toast. But it isn't. You call the waiter. You tell him you ordered buttered toast. He scowls at you. You think he is going to attack you. But that would take too much effort, I suppose, so he growls, loud enough for the room to hear, 'Don't you know there's a shortage of butter?'

"But there is a great day coming. Someday those brothers will want our business. Then when you order buttered toast you'll get buttered toast—with a smile, too. It'll be buttered on the top. It will be buttered on the bottom. And, yes siree, it will even be buttered on the edges."

That "buttered on the edges" is the snap of the whip. Surely it gets a laugh.

Another story Elmer tells has to do with the checking-out times in hotels. He tells this story:

"I went into a hotel and there behind the clerk who registered me in was a sign the size of a house. It said, 'Checking Out Time 6 O'clock.' Just for a gag I asked the man what time I had to check out. He looked at me as if I had gone mad. 'Six o'clock, can't you read?' he growled.

"I got on the elevator and there was another sign, 'Checking Out Time 6 O'clock.'

"I kinda ducked around where I wouldn't see it, and when the elevator stopped at my floor, I got out and started down the hall. All along the hall, at every corner, there were signs reading 'Checking Out Time 6 O'clock.'

"I went into my room thinking, now I'll be free of those signs. But no sir, you guessed it. The first thing that hit me in the eye was a big one which read 'Checking Out Time 6 O'clock.' By this time I was a bit depressed. I sat down on a chair. You know—I was afraid to look in the bathroom."

The last line cracks the whip—but good. It can't help but get a laugh.

I have still another example of snapping the whip: Talking about aptitude tests used in the selection of salesmen, one speaker who was against such tests said, "Why even the psychologists are not interested in them. I know that—let me tell you of an experience. Last fall our sales executives club had a program on aptitude testing. We had invited two psychologists to speak to us. Well, they came, and they both talked. But here is what got me. One of the learned fellows got up and made his talk and sat down. Then the other doctor was introduced and he told his story. And what did the first Ph.D. do while the second was talking? Did he listen with rapt attention? He did not. He went sound asleep. That's how interested he was. Now, it was O.K. for this fellow to go to sleep if he wanted to. The talk was rather dull, a dull talk on a dull subject. So it was O.K. for him to drop off. But here's what I'd like to know. Why did the buzzard have to snore?"

Again, that's cracking the whip. That last line is sure to get a laugh. So whenever you want that laugh, think of cracking the whip.

These examples should help you perfect your storytelling. Study how others do it. Then practice. How will you study storytelling? The books of stories will not help much, unless it has a chapter on how to tell stories. I have about thirty of these books. Some have good chapters on how to tell the stories, but few of the suggestions are specific. They are a lot like the instructions you get with modern machines. The fellow who writes the instructions probably knows how to operate the machine, but nobody can operate it according to his instructions.

Another fault is that the stories are in written language. They are not in a form that can be used for speaking. If you try to tell a story just as it is in the book, you won't do too well. The man who writes the book is usually a writer. Even though he writes the stories as they should be told, the editor may cut out a lot of words which would be considered unnecessary for the written piece but which are needed when the story is spoken.

I have read stenotyped reports of talks I have given. The straight speech material was just as I thought I gave it, but when I came to the stories, I told myself, "I never said it that way." I did, though. I repeated, I allowed my characters to make mistakes in English, I ummed, and ahed. I thought it was mighty terrible in written form. But the stories went over well; the audiences laughed and applauded.

You can check this yourself by telling a story into a wire or tape recorder and playing it back. Use the story as it is printed in the book, and you don't sound like yourself at all. Revise it into words you speak, and see the difference.

The books with collections of stories help in that they give you ideas for stories. You are looking for a story to help you illustrate a certain point. You look through a number of stories in a joke-book and you see a few possibilities, but they don't suggest the point you want to make. Seldom can you find a story that is exactly as you want to use it. Let's say you want to make a talk on economics. You need a couple of stories to liven such a subject. You look in the comic dictionary and you come up with this quote, "Studying economics won't keep you out of the breadline, but at least you will know why you are there." That is on the subject and it sounds rather good, doesn't it? But will that short sentence be enough to give the relief you want? It is like the gag on the comma—it has to be built up. Why not build a story around it, a father and son story, a husband and wife story? Can you see it? Do what I did with the schoolteacher and the children earlier in this chapter.

After you have the story finished, your next job is to tell it a few times to test it out. Tell it to the boys at lunch today and to your wife tonight, and check their reactions. It may not be much of a story; then again it may be good. The boys at lunch may laugh at it quite enthusiastically, but that is no sign it will go well with the audience. I find that some stories that go well with the wife and kids and with the boys at the luncheon table do not do too well when I use them in speeches. You never know until you give them the big test before an audience. But telling them to friends gives you practice in telling the story and in timing.

I find that it is best to try the story on a group without saying I am testing it for a speech. If you explain this beforehand, the listeners will try to criticize and they won't be thinking of the story merely as a funny story. All you want to know is whether a group of ordinary Joes will laugh at it. If the boys at the table laugh, your question is answered.

After you find there is a laugh in the story, you can rehearse it. You may want to memorize part of it. I memorize certain lines in some of my stories. One goes: "After he has talked for a few minutes, everyone in the audience knows that he is up the creek without the proper equipment, but bravely he goes on and on." That line always gets a laugh. It got a laugh the first time I used it. I couldn't figure why—it wasn't an important line in the story—so I memorized the line. Now I use it that way, and every time it gets a laugh. Many speakers memorize the gag line. They get it just so and then they rehearse it and rehearse it until it goes just the same every time. Even though I have told some of my best stories scores of times, I go over them before each appearance. I tell them to myself as I walk back and forth in the hotel room. I like to feel that this rehearsal makes them better.

One thing is certain: if you memorize and rehearse the gag line, you won't forget the point of the story. You will convince the audience that you know what the point is. I have had the embarrassing experience of messing up the gag line in a story, and it is a sad moment. You have told your story—a good story that got laughs before—and here the people are confused, wondering what they are supposed to do. That isn't so likely to happen when you rehearse.

The wire or tape recorder is a good tool to help you practice your stories. Many speakers I know own machines and try out their speeches on them. When you listen to the recording, you can judge how your story will sound to an audience. The recorder is good because you can experiment with that gag line—you can say it three or four ways and decide which is best. You can check the stories, too. Perhaps the one that reads like a gem doesn't sound so well when you tell it.

Another way to learn how to tell stories is to listen to the men who make their living telling stories, in the theater, the night clubs, the movies, on television, and on the radio. Try not to be carried away by the trend of the story, but watch the technique. Each of these performers has spent years learning how to tell stories. Watch his gestures, his facial expressions, and his movements. Note how he uses his voice, now soft, now fast, now slow. Note how he puts in periods and commas, with a wave of his hands or a shrug of his shoulders. Watch his pauses; his change of pace. You can learn a lot from these professionals. Note how they use many of the suggestions given here, and others of their own, too. If you want to tell funny stories, you might as well become a good storyteller, and this kind of study will help.

Now let's review some of these suggestions:

1. Use the funny story or gag to help make a point. Tell your gag and then button up your point.
2. Condition yourself for the story. Live it as much as you can. Dialect will help.
3. Don't laugh before the audience is supposed to laugh.
4. Be prepared for no laugh. Sometimes the listeners will cross you up.

5. Don't tell your story too fast. Let them understand it.
6. Remember the four elements: life, suspense, movement, and a good gag line.
7. Try to use the "one, two, three" technique.
8. Build up anticipation by your manner and what you say.
9. Try to add to the suspense with each new incident.
10. Tell the story in your own words, not the words from the book.
11. Put yourself in the story. If the environment is strange, explain why you were there.
12. Don't go in for the vulgar if it doesn't come naturally.
13. Avoid racial or religious stories; they might offend someone.
14. Study the timing of that gag line. Learn how to get off gag lines before you learn the balance of storytelling technique. Learn how to crack the whip.
15. Practice your stories on all who will listen. Practice will give you a good technique.
16. Listen to the professionals tell stories. Learn their tricks, and use them.

In my talk on "How to Run a Sales Meeting" I have a unit called Don't Be Too Funny. Last winter, in a meeting in Buffalo, I gave this talk in the morning. At luncheon that day, Art Hood, then chairman of National Sales Executives, Inc., was the speaker. At one point in his talk he said, "At this point my notes remind me to tell a funny story. This morning Ed Hegarty told us not to tell funny stories. So just consider that I have told you a funny story, and I'll go on with my talk."

Many speakers could gain by following Art Hood's example. But since not many of you will, I urge you learn how to tell funny stories well.

7

News Takes Some Handling

Audiences like news. You are telling them something they might not know. Why do they read newspapers . . . listen to the radio . . . watch a congressional committee on television? To see what is happening—isn't that why? Because of that interest, news is one of your most effective speech elements.

News comes out of your newspaper, of course, but there is other news, too. How about that new feature of your product, that new angle to your plan, that bit of research, that something you know that the listener doesn't? All are news, and the good speaker uses them. But how?

Let's take that item in this morning's newspaper. Here are a few suggestions:

Talk about the item. You say, "Did you read about the man who . . . ?" You pause, and watch the heads nod.

You talk about the item and hold up a clipping. Your listeners all look at the clipping.

You talk and hold up the page of the newspaper on which the item appeared. The page is larger than the clipping; its size makes the item seem more important.

You produce the whole newspaper, and turn to the page on which the item appeared and show it. This is a build-up from the clipping and the page.

You collect scores of clippings on the subject, and fill an envelope. Then when you want to use them to make your point, you empty the envelope on a table. The audience sees piles of clippings. To be more dramatic, you might fill a large sack with such clippings, or you might even fill a barrel.

Once I heard a speaker telling his audience that the public was becoming conscious of the vitamin content of foods. To prove his point, he brought out a barrel of clippings, emptied the barrel on a table, and read a few of the headlines. "I collected these clippings in the last month," he said. "These articles are telling people just what I have been telling you tonight. That vitamins are important to our health. Listen to this. . . ." He took one clipping and read a part of it. He picked up another and read a headline. He reached into the bottom of the pile and came up with a photograph and described that. He used his barrel of clippings to dramatize his point. And it helped him convince everybody that his subject was in the news.

You know how people respect anything that is printed. Not long ago I was in the office of an air line buying a plane ticket. I wanted to pay by check, but the agent told me that she could not take my check. She suggested that the hotel might cash the check. While we were talking, another young lady behind the desk asked, "Your picture was in the paper yesterday, wasn't it?"

"Yes, it was," I admitted. "Did you recognize me from the photograph?"

"No, I remembered the name. We'll accept your check," she said.

People accept what the newspapers say—even to taking checks. If you have a point you want to make that can be strengthened with an item out of today's newspaper, use it. Remember, all of your audience lives the life you read of in the newspapers. I make a habit of reading the local newspaper before I go out to talk to a group in a town. Many times I get an item I can use. When you read their newspaper, and mention something you saw in it, they respond favorably to you. In a speech recently I asked how many of the audience had seen a certain picture in the newspaper that morning. I asked for a show of hands, and almost everybody had seen the picture. Such a stunt tells the audience that you are the same kind of a person they are. You look at and like the same pictures they do.

You can use news to show that you are alive, in tune with today. Next time you make a speech, mention some angle of Little Orphan Annie's current troubles. Note the response you get. Li'l Abner and Dick Tracy and other comic characters are just as much a part of the life of this group as the butcher or baker. Speak of the comic characters and you are on common ground with your audience. You never heard a stuffed shirt speak in a friendly way of Blondie and Dagwood, did you? If you look at the comics, let them know you do. It helps if your listeners know that you enjoy these characters that are so much a part of the American scene.

In one of my talks on simple language and the use of small words, I asked the audience, "How many of you read the comics? Come on now, everybody who reads the comics hold up your hand, please." About every hand in the room went up. I then make the point that 80 per cent of the words in the comics are one-syllable words. But the show of hands tells me that I am among friends who are friends of my friends, the characters in the comic pages.

Mention, too, the heroes of the sports pages. They have power to help you seem regular. When you go out to lunch during the baseball season, what do the boys talk about? Perhaps you know nothing of baseball, but it doesn't hurt to mention Ted Williams or Bob Feller or Casey Stengel. Remember, that audience has a great interest in sports. Every newspaper has a page or two of sports news, and it is not difficult to pick an item that will get a response.

Unusual stories in the newspapers make good topics. Last winter during the cold weather, a family away for a week came back to find their house full of birds. The birds came down through the chimney. That item was talked over at dinner and luncheon tables all over the state.

I heard a speaker use that item in a speech on Foreign Affairs. He told the story about the birds getting into the house. He told how the homeowner and his family came in to find the birds. Now what were they to do? Get rid of the birds or try to live with them? One neighbor said, "Let's all go home and get our shotguns and start shooting. We'll get them out of here quick." Another said, "Let's open all the windows and shoo them out." Another offered this advice, "Bring in the exterminator. Then tomorrow we can come in and sweep them up."

To each of these men with a plan, the homeowner put one question. To the first, "Have you ever tried to get birds out of a house by shooting at them?" The first adviser had to admit that he hadn't. Of the second the homeowner asked, "Have you ever tried getting birds out of your house by opening the windows and shooing?" The second adviser had to admit that he had not. Then the homeowner asked the other adviser, "Have you ever tried using poison gas in a house to get rid of birds?" And the third man had to admit that he had not. "But my brother-in-law is an exterminator," he said. The homeowner told him, "You seem to be the only man who has some sense in his proposal."

Then the speaker said, "Gentlemen, that is about the way it is with our foreign affairs. We have a lot of advisers telling us what to do but nobody that can guarantee that what they propose will work."

That build-up of a news item shows what can be done with an unusual story taken from a newspaper, and on a subject far afield, too.

You can emphasize the news item by a bit of audience participation. I do that when I ask the question about the comics. Recently, I saw a speaker ask a man from the audience to come up on the stage. When the man was beside him, the speaker said, "This morning before the meeting, Joe Whosis here showed me a clipping out of his home-town newspaper. Joe, do you still have that clipping?"

Joe admitted that he had, and produced the clipping.

"Well, then," the speaker went on, "would you be good enough to read it to us?"

Joe was glad to, and did.

The showmanship of the stunt gave more importance to the news item because it got more attention for it. If it was good enough for Joe to notice on his own, it must be something special.

When you use a bit of news, build up its importance. Perhaps the editor gave it only a few lines on page 7, but if you use it, you must show why the item is important to the listeners. You can do this in a number of ways:

You can say it is important. I heard a speaker say, "This little item took up only ten lines on page seven. It was down at the bottom of the page, buried in cheap advertising, but let me tell you this. That bit is more important in the length of time you will live on this earth than any story in that newspaper today. Get that now —more important in the years you will live." That might be called pouring it on, but you get the idea that the item was important, don't you? The audience did, too.

A second method of making your news item important is to act as if you believe. You must express your conviction and get it over. You have heard the protagonist of a candidate for office. He praises his candidate out of all reason, it seems. You wonder if he believes what he says, but his manner and the energy he throws into his pleas make you feel that he does. One of my sons went with a friend to a meeting of a political club. The next morning he said to me, "Pop, those fellows think that man is a tin god." The man he referred to was the candidate.

"Don't you think he is?" I asked.

"Oh, he's probably O.K.," the boy admitted. "But they think he is something special."

Those speakers got over the idea that they meant what they said. When you speak of your news item, you should try to get some of that spirit.

A third method to impress the audience with the item's importance is to be serious about it. Don't kid it. I heard a speaker trying to prove his point with the spring pastime of one person trying to outdo another in his count of the early robins. He said, "This week everybody in our neighborhood has been counting robins. The first fellow that got into the newspaper said he had seen seven in his back yard. The next night another fellow had seen eleven. But the third night some fellow upped the count to twenty-four. I think he went a little too far, though. He said he saw twenty-four robins, four of them wearing overshoes."

The last line of that story takes it out of the serious. The speaker was kidding his own news—which was all right if he wanted the laugh more than he wanted the group to believe.

Some speakers can get themselves excited about a bit of news. They do it with their voice and the way they act. You have heard Walter Winchell on the radio. He has a tense tone of voice which, added to his speed of delivery, makes the listener feel that what he says is important. Your excitement can add to the importance of what you tell.

You can add to this importance by building up expectancy in the audience. You can do this by what you say, by your manner, by adopting a confidential tone. Any news item can be built up in the same way a story can. There are many suggestions for that on page 38.

News that comes from research is good, but remember that most groups are suspicious of your research. They feel that the research was trying to prove something. When you present facts from research, try to make clear that the research was honestly done. I heard one speaker say, "When we started this survey we didn't know how it was coming out. The people interviewed might have said just the opposite, but they didn't."

It helps if your survey confirms the listeners' opinions, so that they seem to be sitting there saying, "I knew that all the time." Perhaps they never gave the subject a thought, but they know now. If it does not agree with their opinions, admit that you felt as they do before you saw these figures. Then try to explain why you were wrong.

If you have a product to offer as your news item, use an unveiling. I am sure you have heard groups applaud at such unveilings. In making the introduction, use a fanfare—give it the treatment the announcer gives the star of the radio show. Your new product is your star. Dramatize its unveiling. Give it all you can. Raise your voice with that reverence that the master of ceremonies uses for the big star as you whisk away the cloth, raise the shroud, or open the curtain. Let the "ohs" and "ahs" and the applause swell up. Lead the applause yourself if it is slow in coming. You must radiate enthusiasm when you present this new product. Usually every man in that room makes all or a part of his living selling that product, and they have to share your enthusiasm.

You have seen speakers talk through the preliminaries that lead up to the presentation of a product while the product sits beside them in full view. You look at the product and you form your own opinions. If the speaker had kept his product covered until he was ready to present it, he could have suggested the opinions you should have. That's why it is good technique to keep the product covered until you are ready to talk about it.

This idea of an unveiling can be used with any type of subject. Let's say your subject is a fund-raising campaign for a new wing at the hospital. Why not unveil the architect's drawing of the new building at the proper time? If you show the drawing ahead of time, the listeners have time to form opinions about the project: the building is too big, it is in the wrong place, etc. Keep it under cover until you unveil it; then you can tell them what you want them to think. The unveiling has great possibilities for any news you use.

Your news can be made more interesting by putting it in story form. You might tell an anecdote about how you got this news. You might relate some of the gossip you have had with the characters you met on your survey. You might tell what others who had seen your new product say of it.

Study how the picture magazines handle news. Much of the news these magazines use is manufactured. I'm sure you find that they don't run enough pictures on subjects in which you are interested. Yet on other subjects the editor seems to use too many pictures, that is, if you are not greatly interested in those subjects. A golfer would like to see more pictures of golfers; a bird watcher would like to see more pictures of birds. But the magazine has millions of readers, and the editor is trying, as far as possible, to please everybody. That same editor making up a magazine for golfers would fill it with golf pictures. Making up a magazine for bird watchers, he would fill it with birds. When you speak to a group, you are much in the position of the editor of the golf or bird magazine. Your group has certain special interests. You can easily determine what those interests are. And you can slant your news items at those interests.

Develop your news item as fully as you need. Be sure to carry it far enough so that the audience believes. The other day I saw a speaker show a clipping out of a newspaper that reported the number of persons in the county getting unemployment insurance. As he held up this clipping, he said, "These people won't work because they can live on this unemployment insurance." I did not believe that statement, even though the speaker treated it seriously and seemed quite excited about it. To make me believe it, he would have to bring on more evidence. My questions were: How much do these people get from the unemployment people? How many in the family? How well can they live? How much better off would they be if they worked at a regular job? In handling news without backing it up, the speaker had lost my interest in his plea. If your news item is important to the development of your point, develop it until you have the audience nodding agreement. Your news is of little use if the listeners do not believe it.

News is an almost inexhaustible source of speech material. Develop a nose for it, learn how to dig it out, to shape it to your needs, and to present it to the audience.

Let's review these suggestions for handling news:

1. Study the sources of news for something that ties in with your subject. Use the news to help prove a point.
2. If possible, give the news importance by the way you dramatize it in your presentation.
3. Use the popular items of today's news: the comics, the sports pages, and the slang.
4. Study the unusual stories you find in the newspapers. They can make excellent speech material.
5. Make the news item you use important by the way you handle it. Say it is important. Act as if it is important. Be serious about it. Get excited about it.

6. Do some of your own research for news. Try to make this research fair and unbiased.
7. When you have a new product to talk about, try to give it as much news value as possible. Don't pass up an unveiling.
8. When you are talking about a new plan, take the time to explain it fully.
9. Note how the picture magazines handle news. Many of the picture stories are manufactured news. In many cases your speech news is manufactured. The difference is in the wider interests of the magazine audience.

Some wag has said, "There are three kinds of speech material: (1) the important; (2) the unimportant; (3) the things the listeners remember." Your news can be any one of the three. But the audience will not remember your news items if you don't treat them as if they were important, if you don't get excited about them, and if you don't treat them seriously.

8

When You Talk about People

You start talking about people when you begin, "Mr. Chairman, ladies and gentlemen. . . ." You will never find a better interest builder than Mr. and Mrs. and all the others that inhabit this world of ours. Talk about people, and the audience listens; talk about people in the room, and they love it.

You have heard the expression, "I don't care what they say about me so long as they say something." That is not quite true in speechmaking, of course, but talking about people is good speech technique. There are a few rules that will help.

First, when you mention a man in a speech, get his name right and pronounce it right. Some time ago I was waiting for my turn to talk at a meeting while the president of the organization was reading his report. In the report a certain name was mentioned, and a group sitting at one of the tables cheered. I asked the man next to me, "Who are those fellows cheering?"

"They work for this guy," he said.

When I got up to talk, I mentioned that this man had been cheered. I said, "I guess he's the kind of boss that these boys better cheer every time his name is mentioned, or else." The reference fell rather flat. It didn't get the laugh I thought it would. When I was finished, I mentioned this to one of the men. "Oh, you mispronounced his name," my friend said. Because I had mispronounced the name, my gag had fallen flat. If a man has a name that is difficult to pronounce, stay clear of it, unless you have learned exactly how to pronounce it.

When you say anything about a man in the meeting, make it positive. Make it a boost rather than a knock. If you are telling about something that Joe said, say, "Now Joe is one of the best salesmen I've ever met." Joe likes that and so do Joe's friends. A line like the one about the boss who instructed his men to cheer is not good. It might make the boss mad, or it might embarrass his workers. Make anything you say about a person complimentary.

If you tell a story about a man, let him be the hero. You have heard speakers tell anecdotes about the chairman or the man who asked them to talk which put the man in anything but a favorable light.

Sometimes it is well to leave out names. Once I heard a speaker say, "I never read editorials in the newspapers. Editorials reflect the views of the publisher and I know too many publishers. The ones I know have no ideas worth getting into print." The speaker would have been all right if he had stopped there, but he went on: "Take this town. . . ." Then he named the three publishers of the newspapers. "See what I mean?" The last line was not needed. It surely offended some of the editorial readers in the room, not to mention the publishers.

His idea was to show that newspapers did not sway the public in its voting as they once did. His first statement might have been considered correct, but when he added the names he started an argument.

This incident illustrates a good rule to follow in handling names. Don't depreciate. Perhaps you are in a slow burn over the way you have been handled by the chairman or the committee, but when you get your chance to get even—hold everything. I have suffered while the president, the treasurer, and chairmen of sundry committees talked on and put my audience to sleep for me. What I wanted to say about such club management couldn't be printed, but when I got to my feet I acted as if everything was as it should be. The audience likes that better. They say, "They sure pushed him around but he was a good sport about it."

When you say anything about the introduction that the chairman gave you, compliment him on it. You may kid him a bit about it, but do it in a friendly way. Sometimes the introduction you get gives you a pain because it is so lengthy. If you feel compelled to comment on it, use the line I mentioned in Chap. 4, "That sure was a wonderful introduction, wasn't it? It should be, because I wrote it." Perhaps you will not want to take the blame for such an introduction, but remember this—the chairman may have spent a lot of his good time working out that introduction. He was doing it to be kind to you. Why should you be angry about it?

Once a chairman telephoned me long distance twice about what he would say about me in an introduction. He spent his money and put a lot of work into it, but the introduction was mighty sad. Even so, he deserved my thanks and I gave it. You don't make enemies by complimenting a chairman. Remember, he is one of the local group. Boost him, build him up, but never tear him down. Not long ago I heard a speaker say, in kidding the chairman, "I don't know how his wife has managed to put up with his bellyaching as long as she has." The line got a laugh, and the chairman smiled, but I'm sure he didn't like it.

Some speakers have the habit of speaking of the chairman as an old friend. Recently after a meeting I asked the chairman, "How long have you known the speaker?"

"I just met him tonight," the chairman said.

Yet all through his talk the speaker had referred to the chairman as an old friend. I imagine that the audience felt that since the speaker was a friend of the chairman, he was a friend of theirs too. By building up this impression the speaker was getting that group to feel that he was a regular guy, one of them.

When you speak of a man, give a word picture of him if you can. When you report what he said, try to change your voice so that it seems another is speaking. A speaker says, "In that booming, big voice of his he says. . . ." You tend to hear that booming voice, and you feel you can see the man described.

You need people for your anecdotes, and for the gossip with which you build up the anecdotes. Some men are good at using big names. They speak intimately of the great men of today. If you know these big men and associate with them, this may be all right. But you run the chance of having the audience feel you are superior when you say, "I was talking to the senator." You have to remember that the listener does not meet such big shots regularly. Recently I heard a speaker, who was planning to quote the members of a congressional committee, say this, "You may wonder why I came to be talking to these fellows. Well, here is how it came about. . . ." With that introduction he explained how he got his information. Since his explanation was logical, his report carried weight.

I heard another fellow quote a big name and say this, "I met him at a cocktail party. He was coming in as I was going out. I found out later that it wasn't the same party. No, I didn't talk to him direct. I got what he said out of a newspaper."

When you speak of the little names, try to handle them as if you belong. Don't give the idea that you are slumming when you go into a bar. Bartenders, taxi drivers, elevator operators are the kind of people your audience sees every day. When you speak of a shoeshine boy, don't give the idea that you feel you are better than he. The audience doesn't feel that way about their friends.

When you talk about your family, you show that you are one of them. In your talk about your wife, call her "dear" or "honey"; use the pet name because you will say that naturally. Don't be afraid to let the listeners know how you feel about her. You can use the idea that you are the boss but that she runs the place. You can use such lines as, "I'm a normal husband; I do anything I want to do. That is, as long as my wife wants me to." But don't put your wife in the impossible story that you got out of the jokebook. Somehow such stories never seem to come off.

There are some things I have found out about handling your children as speech material. In talking, I usually refer to them as kids or boys (I happen to have only boys); then I identify them as to age. "When my younger boy was sixteen, he took a job delivering ice for the ice company. . . ." I try to give the impression that I am on speaking terms with them. (I am, most of the time.) I may use descriptive phrases, "the smart one" or "the one that speaks correct English" or "the one that leans on the table when he eats." I try to let the listeners know that these kids of mine have just as little respect for me as their youngsters have for them.

Perhaps if you study that paragraph about the kids you will see what those tricks do. They stamp me as a regular dad. Some in the audience are nodding their heads when I talk about the youngster leaning on the table when he eats. Of course, some of that audience have well-behaved children, but that is not true of the majority. And that larger number is your audience.

If you indicated that your children are perfect, the audience wouldn't believe you. What you say may be true, but if it doesn't sound true, it is better not to use the story. Any healthy child can supply a father with plenty of good material—more than he needs. Listeners like to hear you talk about your kids.

Relatives are good subjects, but try to make your remarks complimentary, even in regard to the in-laws. If the joke is on your mother-in-law, say something nice about her. "Sure, she's bossy, but she buys all the kid's clothes. I can stand a little bossing for that. In fact, twice as much as she dishes out." Your wife's brother who is always borrowing—mention him if you want, but add the line that makes him regular: "Oh, he always pays me back." Relatives are good material, but don't run them down. It may give the audience the idea that you are unhappy, and listeners do not like unhappy speakers. Of course, you can be unhappy about your competitor, the party in power, or about how your cause is being neglected by the city officials, but don't appear unhappy about your home life.

When you speak of the neighbors, boost them, too. The old fellow who crabs all the time about your dog—tell them about his crabbing but excuse him by saying, "I guess the old guy's got a lot to crab about—living next to me" or "Maybe I'd be crabbing too, if I lived next to me." Build up the neighbors, but build yourself up, too. I tell one story that does that:

Last summer a new family moved in next door to us. They had two children, a boy, three, and a little girl, two. Now it has been a long time since we have had anything to do with young children, so we decided, my wife and I, that no matter what the little children did we would take it in stride—without screaming.

Now children of that age are just too young to understand. You can tell them about pulling flowers or breaking milk bottles or turning on the hose, but it does no good. Their family did that, but still it did no good. They broke our milk bottles and they turned on our hose. My wife started to keep the milk bottles inside, and she had some luck in talking them out of turning on the hose.

One day she was upstairs and she heard the little girl say, "Turn on the water, Carl." The little girl couldn't reach the water.

My wife came out on the porch deck, looked down on the two, and asked, "What did you want Carl to do, Chris?"

The little two-year-old girl looked up at her. "Turn on the water," she said. Turning to the boy, she said, "Turn on the water, Carl."

My wife now decided to use some of her child psychology. "Would your mother like it if you turned on the water?" she asked.

Chris shook her head as she said, "Turn on the water, Carl."

Carl still looked from one to the other.

"Wouldn't your mother punish you if you turned on the water?" my wife asked.

Chris nodded. "Turn on the water, Carl," she said.

I use that story to prove that psychology is a great thing if it works; but that it doesn't always work. Note how it follows the rules: it doesn't criticize anybody and it builds us up as regular people. Yet it is about real people. If you have been using critical stories about the neighbors, try cutting out the criticism. You will find that they go over better.

The boss and the associates at the office make up another group that can be used. The rules are pretty much the same. If you have to make the point that the credit manager down at the office is an old so-and-so, add, "If I had to look at figures for eight hours per day, I'd go nuts." Try to use stories about these characters that put them in a good light. You might say, "Most of the time he is an old so-and-so, but he's got me out of a lot of jams." Get the idea?

If you are going to mention the boss, better make it complimentary. Even though the boss may laugh at your wisecrack, he may also list you as one of the expendables. In Chap. 6, I use the line, "I don't think the boss would like me to tell this." You have heard speakers do that with the boss sitting in the audience. You have heard them add, "Stop me, Mr. Boss, if you don't want me to tell this." You have probably never heard the boss stop the speaker. If you are planning such a stunt, arrange it with the boss beforehand. The device is good; it makes the listeners feel that this is top-secret stuff. But it is better to set it up beforehand.

If you handle what you say about every person you mention as if that person were your boss, you will surely be safe. I gave that advice to a fellow not long ago, and he said, "That's easy, Ed, I won't mention them." That's not what I mean. I mean treat them courteously, compliment them, build up, but don't tear down. The insult type of story gets a laugh, but it is no good when you are speaking about the family, the wife, the neighbors, the boss, or the associates at the office.

When you quote these persons, try to use their language. This doesn't mean that when you quote what your wife says you try to hit a high falsetto. Use her words. If she calls you "Pop," you might put that pet name in the quotation. If her pet expression is "Dear me!" use it. You probably will approach her tone of voice when you say it.

Of course, the big character in your stories is you. Try to make that "you" a rather humble, old-shoe type of character. Speak in simple language; depreciate your abilities; let the other fellow best you; give him the gag line; let the joke be on you. Perhaps you don't think of yourself as a character, but to this group you are whatever you want to make yourself. You can build up or tear down.

Nobody wants to appear to be a stuffed shirt. O.K., what better way to make a group of listeners feel you are a regular guy than to people your talk with ordinary persons such as they know. If you show by your illustrations that you live and get along with regular people, then why shouldn't you be thought of as regular?

Thus, you have two problems in speaking about people—about yourself and the people around you: (1) Don't build yourself up too much. (2) Keep the others in a good light; always build them up.

Now let's review these suggestions for handling people.

1. When you speak of a person at the meeting, get his name right and pronounce it right. If the name is difficult to pronounce, make the remark about another fellow.
2. Put the person you speak of in a good light, always.
3. Make the other fellow the hero.
4. Don't depreciate in anything you say about a character. Try to find that one thing to compliment.
5. Try to be human in speaking of your wife, your children, or your in-laws. Make them the smart ones and you the one that doesn't catch on.
6. Treat the neighbors kindly. Explain away their shortcomings.
7. Watch how you speak of the boss and the associates at the office. You need the job, and you have to work with those others. Build them up, always.
8. In quoting others, try to speak as they speak. Use expressions they use, and your stories will have more reality.
9. Watch how you handle that most important person—you. Try to keep him natural. It may be difficult, but do what you can.

An audience is made up of people. Nothing interests them as much as other people. They like the man who speaks about the people they know. So give the people in your life a job in your talks.

9

Shoes and Ships and the Rest

Life is just one thing after another. Things are a part of your life, and they are a part of the life of your listeners—the same things too: washbowls, safety razors, electric lights, and mirrors. Speak of any one of them and you are on common ground. The good speaker speaks of the commonplace. Why? Because any audience knows the commonplace.

Many men have a great fear of getting up and giving a talk to a group. Some authorities say that this fear is based to some extent on the fact that the speaker doesn't know what he is talking about. That is why in the first session of a public-speaking class the student is asked to give a short talk on himself or his business—he should know either subject. If a man's fear of speaking is based on his lack of knowledge of his subject, he should have more confidence when he deals with the commonplace. That button on your overcoat, for instance: you know it, it is an old buddy, an old friend. When you speak of it, you are at home, on ground you know; you sound real, natural, human.

Good speakers use these common things; they know them; the audience knows them. But there is another reason why they are good speech material: they can be used to make you seem like a regular fellow to your listeners. How can you help liking a speaker who talks about the shiny pants of his blue-serge suit? He explains that when he makes a talk he always wears this blue serge. But tonight when he took the pants off the hanger, he noticed this shine on the seat. It had been there for some time, but tonight he noticed it. So he put on the pants and went downstairs to the wife and said, "Honey, look at the seat of these pants, will you? Do you think that shine will show?"

Now he reports what the little woman said. "Not if you don't take off your coat," she says. A speaker can go on and on with that, can't he? For that has happened in your home and mine, and if it hasn't happened we can imagine it happening. So you like that fellow, don't you?

Of course such a story should help you make a point. To illustrate, here is a story I tell about Pat Kelley's dog and a list of the points I have made with it in different speeches.

"We were out playing bridge with the Kelleys, the Missus and I. This was before we found out that Canasta was a game better suited to people with our mental capacity. Of course, in an evening out the hostess always serves something to eat. This night it was popcorn. Mrs. Kelley brought out a big bowl of it and put it in the middle of the table. Now I like popcorn. As I saw it coming, I thought, 'This is wonderful. How'd she know that popcorn is my favorite fruit?'

"Now Pat had a big, sad-eyed dog, and this giant mutt was sitting beside me. As we played cards, I looked down at him every now and then, but the mutt appeared to be asleep. I patted him a few times and let it go at that. But the mutt must have smelled that popcorn, for when I reached out for my first handful, and got that handful started to my mouth, the dog slapped me with his paw. I looked at the dog and those sad eyes. I looked at the corn in my hand with my mouth watering, and you know what happened? I fed the corn to the dog.

"As soon as he got the corn, I reached for the bowl again. One for me and one for him, I thought. But the mutt had different ideas, for just as I was about to toss the corn into my open mouth, he slapped me again. I looked at the dog and said, 'Look, Rover, this ain't funny.' But the look in his eye decided me. He got the second helping.

"While this was not amusing to me, it was greatly so to the host and hostess and to the little lady that came with me. I took about six handfuls of that popcorn, and I never got one of them. I tried speeding up, but it was no go. Just when I would start them to my mouth, the dog would slap me with his paw. I'd give him the popcorn, rub the sore spot on my leg, and try again.

"Now the others were eating the corn, and were having a high time, enjoying the corn, and me too. I said to myself, 'I should be smarter than this dog.' And so I tried ignoring the bowl of popcorn. But that did not work either. When the mutt was ready for more corn, he slapped me with that paw. By this time my bridge-playing companions were lying in the aisle, so to speak, and I decided to stop it all.

"I said, 'Well, Rover, we'll fix this.' I took the bowl of corn and laid it on the floor beside the dog.

"I was pretty proud of myself just then. I had fixed this thing once and for all. But did the dog eat that corn? He did not. He looked at it; he looked at me. Then he got up and went out of the room."

I use that story to make a number of points, one point to a speech. Here they are:

That today people want things handed to them.

That sometimes when you think you are smart, even a dog is smarter than you are.

That you have to give service or that customer will walk out on you.

Stories of this type have scores of point-making possibilities.

The office is good for a number of such stories: your desk and the things on it; the clean-up drives the boss puts on; your chair that squeaks when you turn in it; your secretary who tries to place the things in your office the way she wants them.

Here is one I use on that theme.

"As I travel around the country making speeches, the clubs take a lot of photographs of me. I always have these sent to me, and I put them on a big board I have in the office.

"This board with the photos offends the sense of neatness of my secretary. Time and again she asks me if it would be all right to rearrange the photos on the board.

"Since I can figure a woman's ulterior motive from miles away, I always tell her I like them as they are. But she keeps boring in. Every month she comes in with a new idea. But I, too, have a secret weapon. I say, 'How about that copy work I gave you yesterday?' For over two years that device worked.

"Then about four months ago I was away for three weeks. I guess in that time she ran out of copy work, for when I came back, she proudly showed me the office. The board was cleaned off, all but a few of the pictures. I said, 'Aw, nuts.'

"She said, 'Before you say anything, I want you to promise to leave this office as it is for one month. I put all those old photos in this folder. If you ever want any of them they'll be here.'

"I said, 'Look, why didn't you leave them as they were?' She had taken down 90 per cent of them. The ones she had left were not the ones I would have selected.

" 'But it looks so much neater now,' she said.

" 'Yeah, but I liked it the other way.'

" 'I'll tell you what,' she said, 'you leave it this way for a month. I'll bet you'll like it better this way.'

"It's been that way for two months now. And I don't like it better. But I'll tell you this. I'm still making speeches, and I'm still getting photos, and I'm putting them up on that board. Give me time, and I'll have it covered again."

Such a story goes over big. Why? Because all of that audience have offices; they all have secretaries. They know how helpless they would be without these girls. They know how they have to give up the pictures on the wall or the arrangement of chairs, or how they have to put up with a growing plant in the office just to keep peace in the family. If your story shows them that you have similar problems, they feel that you must be O.K.

I use that story to make the point that the usual big-shot executive is run by his secretary. It makes that point, and it also helps cut me down to a size more acceptable to the group.

You could make other points with it. How about these?

Don't waste time battling the inevitable.

Women are smarter than we are.

What I like you don't like.

To get along with people let them have their way.

Of course, stories about things can be used to explain. Recently I heard a speaker say, "I won't be able to stand up straight while I speak to you tonight. Last week end I put down some asphalt tile in my basement rumpus room. I guessed I stretched a little bit. I don't think my back will ever straighten again."

Projects around the house are good, for most homeowners have done them. If you have no projects, you probably flick ashes on the new carpet when the Missus isn't looking. Mention that and you make friends.

But while you make these friends, try to make your point, too. Making friends is one of the objectives, but the big objective is putting over your story. Therefore check your anecdotes about small things. See if you can't slant the telling of them so they help you make that point a bit stronger.

Here are some suggestions for using these things in your speech:

Don't Show Off. Perhaps you want to talk about your Cadillac; you have a good story about it, but remember that most of the listeners don't own Cadillacs. You should always try to whittle yourself down to their size. When you speak of the things about you, avoid being boastful. Last month I heard a speaker do that with his Cadillac. He mentioned that he had a Cadillac. Then he explained it this way: "Yes, I own a Cadillac. The kids call it 'the scow.' You know, all my life I have wanted to own a Cadillac. I have felt that it would make me one of these men of distinction. Well, I worked and slaved and saved, and now I own one. It's a 1940 job, long and black. It cost me about two hundred bucks more than a 1940 Chevy, but I got it. I'm a Cadillac driver—what make of car do you drive? And so tonight I can stand here and casually mention that Cadillac of mine. Makes you think I'm hot stuff, doesn't it?"

The speaker knew the rule; he was trying to show his audience that his problems were similar to theirs.

Explain. If you have a possession that sets you apart from others, and you want to speak of it, explain how you came by it. The man with the Cadillac did that. Don't say that you have two cars without explaining that the other belongs to your brother-in-law who is in the Army. If you have a pedigreed pup, explain how you got it. If you have a Saint Bernard, tell how it eats you out of house and home, but explain that if you get rid of it the kids will vote you out. In your pet stories, better make the dog a common mongrel, a cross between this and that. Then the fellow who has a pedigreed pup can feel a bit superior.

Talk it down. I have a friend who has an eighteen-room house. It is a beautiful place, completely done over, furniture, carpet, drapes, and all, but here's what he says about it in his speeches. "This home of mine is a modest eighteen-room shack on a couple of acres of not too well-kept lawn. In the winter we have to close up six of the rooms, for we can't afford to heat all of it. The Missus says she likes bigness, and boy, have we got that. We've been living in the place for four years now and we haven't yet finished an inventory of what has to be done to make it livable. The Missus bought it while I was away on a trip. She had a purpose. You see, I'm a lazy guy; like to sit down when I get home. Ever since we've been married I've been promoting an easy chair as a Christmas present for me, and what do I get—an eighteen-room house with fixing needed in every room. Now when I mention that easy chair she says, 'With a house like this, what do you want with an easy chair?' "

Note how the speaker makes himself one of you by the way he speaks of that big house. Perhaps nobody in the audience has an eighteen-room house, or wants one after the speaker gets through, but the speaker's idea is to sell himself, not the house.

Use the Familiar. Talk about things they know. If you have a story about buying a jack plane, change it to a story about a screw driver. They all know screw drivers. Familiar things are like the poor—they are all around you. Why go far afield for material when the knife on the end of your watch chain might make a story just as good? You may say, "That's O.K., but don't unfamiliar things have more interest?" I doubt that they do. The familiar is common to you and to the group. You know these common things. When I speak of my pen that leaks, I see that pen, I feel it, I see the ink on my fingers. How could I be unnatural in speaking of it? The other night I saw a speaker show an ink spot on his hand; he held up the hand with the ink spot. With the other hand he held up the pen and asked, "How can the little cartridge in that ball-point pen leak that much ink? What would have happened if I had bought one of the fifty-cent pens that the slick salesman tried to sell me? If this much ink could spill out of a twenty-nine-cent pen, how much ink can spill out of a fifty-cent one—twice as much?" Was there anyone in the audience that didn't know what this man was talking about? Every one of them had probably tried to wash ink off his hands after using a pen. Everyone had probably had that same question: "Where did it all come from?" What was the man using this story for? He was making the point that appearances are deceiving.

In speaking of common things, don't give the impression that you are an old crab. Say, "That dog—I complain about him a lot, but, you know, I think he really likes me. And if the Missus would suggest getting rid of him, I'd probably be the first to scream."

Remember, these small things appeal to the audience. Think back to the last talk you heard. What is it that you remember? Isn't it some little thing? Men who heard me speak months before remind me of some trivia that I mentioned. They ask, "Still got that leaky pen?" or "Where's your red necktie?" To these questioners I have a habit of asking, "Do you remember the point that I made with that pen?" Usually, the man thinks an instant and then tells me. The trivia interested him, and it helped me get the point over.

Always Button Up Your Point. When you use the small thing to make a point, emphasize the point. State the point, bring up your small thing to illustrate the point, and then restate the point. There is little sense in bringing in your old overalls if you don't make a point with them. But make sure that the audience knows what you are trying to do with the illustration. The best way is to tell them what you are going to do, and then retell them after you have used the illustration. Don't get so lost in your story about the small things that you forget to button up your point.

One of my speaker friends says, "It's better to use something common and ordinary to make an important point. Use something big or colossal and your point may be lost in the illustration."

Now let's review these suggestions for handling the commonplace in your speaking:

1. Speak of the little things you know well, and some of the fear of speaking to a group vanishes.
2. Use your illustrations with small things to make points.
3. Don't allow your illustrations to put you in the light of a show-off. Never let them help you brag.
4. If the object mentioned is a Cadillac or a yacht, explain it in a way that cuts you down to the size of the audience.
5. Use the familiar in all of your illustrations. If you have a choice between a pencil and a diesel locomotive, select the pencil. The audience will understand that better.
6. Speak of all these things with high regard. You love them all. To you they are a laugh. Don't give the audience the idea that you and these things don't get along so well together.
7. Always make sure that you button up the point you are making with the story about your old tweed coat. State the point, talk about the tweed coat, and then restate the point.

Learn to talk about things. Men have told me, "Ed, I don't feel right when I am talking about these personal things."

My advice is to get over that feeling. Let's say your point is pure theory. Talk about it directly, and you may be over their heads. Illustrate your point with stories about simple things, and you bring it closer to their understanding. You know these things and the audience likes to hear you speak of them. To prove this, all you need do is listen to the good speakers. Note how much they use trivia. If you are going to be a good speaker, small things will be one of your best speaking tools.

10

That Old Debbil Figures

Perhaps you have seen an audience stand up to cheer a speaker when he finished his talk. But it wasn't a speaker who used too many figures. For no matter how good you are as a speaker, your figures will be the deadliest part of your talk.

You may love figures; you may be able to quote the batting averages of every man who hits over .300 in both major leagues. You may know your statistics so well you can spout figures for hours on end. But your liking for figures is not shared by most listeners. In fact, they will like you better if you leave your figures at home.

The other night a speaker said, "Now I am forced to bore you with some statistics." Another speaker said, "I have a good talk here—all except the part that is loused up with statistics." Both were on the beam—they knew how any audience feels. In my talk "How to Get Better," there is a unit called Use Your Big Mouth. When I show the chart with this wording on it, I ask the audience, "What is the first rule on using your big mouth?" Invariably someone calls, "Keep it shut." I agree, and that admonition might be good advice for the man who is about to quote statistics.

But if you have figures to quote and must use them to prove your point, what then? In my book *How to Write a Speech,* I give some suggestions for preparing the statistics you plan to use. Now I'll try to give you some ideas on speaking them.

The best alternative to no statistics is to use as few as possible.

Not so long ago I heard a speaker say, "In this talk I have only one statistic. Here it is—I'm going to talk for five minutes." A speaker who uses too many statistics seems to be claiming too much. If you use one figure—let's say it is the sales of your company last year—your listeners may remember it. Use two figures—let's say the second is the amount of profit your company made—and you double the listeners' job. As you increase the number of figures, you tax the memory more.

In using figures, what is your purpose? Do you want to impress, inform, or what? Once you have that purpose clearly stated, you can better determine what figures to use and how many. Once I worked with a speaker on a script. He had a sheet of figures that he wanted to use. I knew that if he used them he would bore the audience.

"Do you have to use all these?" I asked.

"Yes, every one of them," he said.

We rehearsed the talk with the figures. About halfway through the sequence, he stopped. "I believe we could cut out some of these," he said.

He started again with about half of his figures. Again he stopped. In the end he used just one out of the whole page of figures. When he analyzed what he was trying to do, he found that he could do the job without the figures. And his speech was better without them. Figure out the job you want the statistics to do, and then use the ones that will do that job.

Next try to trim the details off your figures. Skip the odd cents, the odd dollars, the odd years. Talk in round figures. One million instead of 991,293. Use as few as possible, and trim the ones you use. If you have charts, spell out round numbers: one million, two million, etc.

If you use the numerals and the ciphers, the audience needs more time to catch on. Even though you have figures for the forty-eight states, use the figures for a typical state and say that the others are about in the same relation. You don't have to overwhelm your listeners to make them believe.

Another device is to put people in your figures. A million

dollars is a lot of money. Recently I heard a speaker say, "This project is wasting one million dollars of the taxpayers' money. But nobody gets excited over one million dollars any more." The speaker could have stopped there, but he put a friend in his figure and said, "The other day I asked a friend, 'When I say one million dollars, what do you think of?' The friend said, 'Those politicians in Washington.' " Here is another use of people: "All the people in the state of Ohio could have a bath in a giant bathtub if the 405 million gallons of water used in our factory here were pumped into it." That impresses you as a lot of water, doesn't it?

Another way to make your figures easy to take is to compare with the familiar. If you say that your factory uses lots of paint each day, it may mean one gallon or ten to the listener. Tell him that you paint over one-half million square feet every day and he still may have a hazy idea. Explain that you use enough white paint to paint 133 six-room houses every day, and perhaps he gets a better idea. You may say that you have over one hundred thousand windows in your factory. That is a lot of windows, isn't it? But can you picture one hundred thousand windows. Say that the cost of cleaning those windows just once is over twelve thousand dollars, and your listener whistles. He also gets a better picture. By comparing with the familiar you make the figures clearer.

You can put your figures into anecdotes. Perhaps you have heard the story about the man who appeared at the office of the automobile factory and asked the executive who greeted him, "You run a car off your assembly lines here every minute, I'm told. Is that true?"

The executive admitted that it was.

"Ever run a car off faster than that?" the visitor asked.

"Yes, last year for a time," the executive said, "we were running one off every thirty seconds."

"Thirty seconds," the visitor said. "I musta got one of them."

The story gives an idea of speed of manufacture, doesn't it?

Any figures used should be localized if possible. The events in news from the other side of the world are of less interest than those at home. Explain that your figures mean X dollars for this town or this county. Let's say you use the income per capita in some remote part of the world, then give it for a state in another part of the country, and then in my state. Now I am listening. Get your data as close to the chair I am sitting in as you can.

It is a good idea to explain what the figures mean per person. Let's say you have a suggestion system in your factory. You pay the workers for suggestions that save material or cut costs or increase safety. You might say, "Last year we paid out over thirty thousand dollars for suggestions to about two thousand employees." You might make that, "Last year we paid out over twenty bucks for every suggestion accepted. How many of those twenty-dollar bills did you get?" Recently I heard a speaker say, "You have a wife and two kids, haven't you? O.K., then multiply this figure by four. That's all you will have to pay." Of course, everybody does not have a wife and two children, but the illustration is so clearly put that any member of the audience can figure his share. Your audience can picture a man, a family, a crowd, perhaps even one hundred persons; but ask them to see more and you ask too much. If possible, explain the figure in terms of what it means to the listener.

Even though your figures are loaded, try to be fair. When you use figures, you usually want the listeners to write their congressmen, storm the city hall, buy your package, or get steamed up about your cause. One good way to appear fair is to quote your figures, and then ask, "What do you think?" Your question brings them into the discussion. You make it seem that they are making your conclusion for you.

Another way to seem fair is to give the source, the authority, and the basis. When a listener sees a figure that is new to him or that startles him, he questions it. If your authority is the Republican National Committee, state that it is. You have heard the political orator say, "These aren't my figures. They don't come from the GOP. No, they are from the Democratic National Committee." When you can quote the opposition, your data have power. It is always better to use figures from an unbiased source, but figures are seldom put out by a group with no ax to grind.

When you give the other fellow a break in your figures, you have a better chance of convincing the listeners that you are fair. But don't give this break without mentioning it and explaining it. If you don't, the audience might not understand that you are bending over backward to be fair. Remember this too—always in an audience there are a few who can outfigure you, even with your own figures.

Make any figure you use seem important. If it isn't important, why talk about it? You say that there are 743 parts in this product you make in the factory. Then you say, "Why is that figure important? Well, last year there were 1,123 parts, and the year before that 1,365 parts. In two years we have cut the parts count almost in half. Isn't it good old horse sense that a machine with half as many parts will give better service?" State that your figure is important; then explain why.

Always know the details of your figures. Many times a speaker fancies a figure and uses it in his speech. When he is asked about it, he can't explain the details. If you don't know the basis or the authority for a figure, leave it out of your speech. After a talk not long ago, I asked a speaker where he got a figure. "I don't know," he said, "but it sure helps prove my point, doesn't it?" The figure did that, but after that admission I didn't believe any part of the man's talk.

It is easier to put over your figures if you give the listeners something to look at. Write your figures on a blackboard; make up charts; ask the audience to write them down; pass out a table from which the audience can read them. Any such visual device will help make your figures important and will help get them remembered.

Figures aren't popular, with speakers or with listeners. If you have to use them, here are some suggestions in brief:

1. Use as few figures as possible.
2. Stick to your objective. Don't bring in figures because you have them. Use them only to do what you want them to do for you.

3. Cut all details. When you use figures, trim off all the odd dollars, odd cents, and odd years. The listeners will remember only the big figure anyway.
4. Use them with people. Use stories, gossip and names to make the figures understandable. A million dollars means one thousand persons paying one thousand dollars apiece.
5. Compare with the familiar. One dollar buys one hundred lollipops. Perhaps I know lollipops better than I do dollars. If so, talk to me in terms of lollipops.
6. Localize. Put the figures on a local basis—my county, my town, my family.
7. Explain what they mean to the listener. He sits there asking, "What does this mean to me?" Tell him in terms of his taxes, his family, his car.
8. Try to seem fair. Don't use figures that you have faked up to prove your point. Somebody can usually check your figures.

These suggestions are designed to put some life into your figures. It is a mighty discouraging job. You will be a happier speaker without figures and you will speak to a happier audience.

II

Surely Some Dramatics

It was the fifth session of the public-speaking class. The instructor asked how many of the men had never made a formal speech in public. Six of the students held up their hands. The instructor asked them to come up front. He asked them to take off their coats. Then he asked them to stand on their heads. Five of them said they couldn't do it. The sixth managed the stunt easily. The instructor insisted that the other five try. They did, but none of them succeeded.

Then the instructor asked one of them, "Can you raise your arms?" The man said he could, and demonstrated. He asked the others to do the same. All of them did. He asked them to wave their hands, to smile, to shake their heads, and to do a little dance. After a number of such exercises, he asked all but one of the men to sit down.

"Why couldn't you stand on your head?" the instructor asked this individual.

"Because I never learned how, I guess," the man replied.

"Did you feel a bit foolish when you were up here trying to stand on your head before the class?" the instructor went on.

"I sure did."

"Did you feel foolish when you waved your arms?"

"No."

"Or when you smiled?"

"No."

"Or when you did that dance?"

"Some, but not too much."

Then the instructor addressed the class: "I may not be able to teach you to stand on your heads when you make a speech, but I do hope that from now on you'll put a little more body action into your speeches."

The instructor had tackled one of the most difficult phases of public speaking. You can get men to write speeches and to deliver them, but those same men won't let themselves go before an audience. Most good speakers seem to have the knack of throwing themselves into their talks.

In the title of this chapter I use the word "dramatics." Perhaps that is not the right word, but I think of the simple wave of your hands, as you ask a question of your audience as a bit of acting on your part. I don't differentiate between these simple gestures and such stunts as untying your bow tie or putting on a funny hat. To me, both are a part of your act. This movement helps you hold the interest of your audience. Most listeners like to see you make a fool of yourself.

But the speaker who puts on the act doesn't feel that he is making a fool of himself. He has a purpose, and as long as he gains his objective, who is making a fool of whom? Yet again and again I have had inexperienced speakers tell me, "Ed, I feel foolish doing such stunts. I'm no actor." To that my stock question is, "You're not a public speaker either, are you?"

"That's for sure," is usually the answer.

"Well, then, aren't you doing a bit of acting when you stand up and speak to a group?" I ask. "Why not go the whole way and give them a bit of play-acting with your words of wisdom?"

Even the simplest gestures help add interest. The other night at a meeting of a Toastmasters Club, I watched a speaker do a one-minute extemporaneous speech. His hands betrayed his nervousness. He had them at his side, in his pockets, and clasped behind him, three positions in one minute, all obviously uncomfortable. I don't mean to say that speakers can't put their hands in any of these positions and be comfortable, but this one made you feel that his hands were worrying him. Now, wouldn't it be well for that fellow to develop three or four gestures? He does such a talk almost every week. He could use one gesture in the first fifteen seconds, another in the second quarter, a third in the third, and the final one in the last quarter. With such a plan he would be worrying about what he did with his hands, rather than with what to do with them.

What four gestures could he use? He could point with one hand. He could shake his fist. He could hold both hands palms up as he asked a question. He could push both hands away from him as he answered the question in the negative. Then why couldn't he nod his head in the affirmative, or shake it in the negative. He could hold both hands clasped above his head as if he were shaking hands with the crowd. Those are but a few of the gestures he could use. But supposing that he planned all of them, and rehearsed them in front of the mirror at home. He might be nervous when he got to his feet, but with four gestures he would have part of his talk ready, and that preparation would help him in his presentation.

Why four gestures? I have a friend who uses one. He shakes his fist at the audience. When he does that over and over, the group may get the idea that they must do what he asks or else. If that man had four gestures, he would give no such impression. Two would be better than one, three better than two. It is easy to learn a number of gestures. You can use your hands, your head, your shoulders, when you are up on a stage. Where the audience can see your feet, you can use them too. There is no reason why you should not have a variety.

Let's say you develop a gesture for use when you do these things:

1. Emphasize an important point. You might slap your right hand into your left; hit the table or lectern with your hand.
2. Ask a question. You might pause and hold your hands out, palms upward. Your facial expression could help you ask the question.
3. State that something is not right. This gesture must show

you feel strongly about this point. You might shake your fist.

4. Ask for action. You might stretch out your arms to indicate they should join you in the activity.

Note that in all these suggestions I say, "you might." Any gesture you use has to be fitted to your physical make-up. The other day I saw a man pound his fist into his hand, but his hands looked frail. A man with large, strong hands can make that gesture much more effectively. Later the same speaker indicated he was grabbing this evil in his hands and shaking the life out of it. Those frail hands didn't seem capable of shaking the life out of any important evil. That's why I say, "you might." Fit your gestures to your looks. Don't get tough with your gestures if you don't look like a person who might get too rough. Try to find a gesture that fits your physique and your personality.

No matter what gesture you use, forget yourself. If you are steamed up about your subject, you will gesture without knowing it. I have photographs that prove that I get my hands up above my head when I am speaking enthusiastically before an audience. If you asked me, I'd say I never raise my hands above my head.

In time you will come to use gestures naturally. You will use them when the speech calls for them. At first, when you try gestures you may overdo them. With experience you will learn how to use them subtly—a gentle wave of the hand throws one idea away, a slight shake of the head indicates that another will not work. But don't wait until you become expert before you start using gestures. Use them early in your speaking career, and learn to use them right by practice. If you are an experienced speaker, check the gestures you use: Do you have a variety? Are they expressive, in harmony with the idea you want to express? Are they planned? Do you use enough?

From the gesture you can go on to play-acting. Recently I saw a speaker pretend that he had forgotten what he was to say about a point. He started once, then again, and to the group it seemed that he was fumbling, trying to get back on the subject. Of course they laughed at his discomfiture. He had set up a guessing game for them. Some thought he had forgotten; others thought it was a gag. After I have done a stunt like that, listeners have asked me, "Ed, did you really forget or was it just a stunt?" I never answer that question. I ask, "What do you think?"

A stunt like this is good for emphasizing a point. I heard a speaker repeat a point he had conveniently forgotten three times. He said, "This part is made of nitrided steel. Excuse me while I repeat it; I don't want to forget it. This part is made of nitrided steel. This part is made of nitrided steel." He buttoned up the stunt by asking, "You know, after you mention that point two or three times, you see how powerful it is, don't you?"

The action in any such stunt is more interesting than your talk. Did you ever notice what happens when someone tries to open or close a window in the room in which you are speaking? The speaker loses all attention. The fellow shutting the window is more interesting than anything the speaker can say.

Thus when you raise your hands the group watches the hands. Even the fellow who is a bit drowsy blinks and looks at you. If you untie your necktie, he sits up straight. If you take off your coat, he wonders if he should take off his.

Any bit of histrionics adds variety. It is difficult to listen to even the experienced speaker as he talks on and on. That is why the best speakers add some stage business.

You may say, "This is all right, Hegarty, but I still feel silly doing any of these stunts."

Let's analyze that statement. Can you smile at an audience? That's acting, isn't it?"

Can you use your hands? Can you put them in your pockets? Can you clasp them behind you? O.K., then why can't you get those hands out in front of you? Why can't you use them for gestures? I try to keep my hands in front of me. I try to keep them moving. I try to keep from using the same gestures over and over. In one of my talks, I pick up a deck of cards and shuffle them. All eyes are on those cards because they think I am going to do a card trick. In another bit I give a selling talk on a pencil and I am surprised at the attention I get when I bring out that pencil and start to talk about it. In this demonstration I do these things:

I hold the pencil in both hands as I show it.

I turn it to show the size of the lead.

I try to pull off the brass eraser holder on the end.

I take the eraser out of the holder and show it.

Is there anything that you couldn't do in that demonstration? I doubt it. In your next talk try a number of these simple things: Use a more elaborate gesture; take something out of your pocket and show it; do a short demonstration such as the one with a pencil. When you are able to do these stunts gracefully, try fumbling as you try to get that newspaper clipping out of your pocket, or drop the pencil on the table a few times during the demonstration. In my talk on public speaking I do this stunt:

I try to show the group a newspaper clipping that is in a leather folder in my inside coat pocket. I manage to have trouble getting the folder out of my pocket. I complain about the way the suit is made. I get a pencil caught in the lining. I finally get the folder out, and then I have so many papers in the folder that I can't find the clipping. I say, "This is not the way to do this. You should have everything ready." By this time the audience has caught on and is laughing.

A beginner couldn't do that stunt without practice. Usually that is the difference between the experienced speaker and the novice. The older fellow can do these stunts with finesse. Two years ago, one month apart, I heard two different speakers do the same talk. One was a young man in his twenties; the other a man in his fifties, pupil and teacher. The talk had stunt after stunt. I saw the young man do the talk first. He was good; he got his points over and he got his laughs. Then a month later I saw the teacher do the talk. Here was the master. He said the same words and did the same stunts, but his experience showed in his timing, in his delivery. When he had finished, I said, "What a performance!" If you are serious about being a good speaker, start putting a bit of this play-acting into every speech. In time you will be able to do it well.

When you do a stunt, take your time. The listeners have to understand what you are doing. You are trying to illustrate a point, not hurrying to get through. Milton Kalisher, a refrigeration engineer, demonstrates that the refrigerant used in his refrigerator is nonpoisonous. He fills a beaker with the gas, explaining that it is heavier than air. He drops some cherries in the liquid. He explains that almost immediately the cherries freeze solid. He takes two of the frozen cherries out of the gas. He says they are frozen solid. He dashes them to the floor, and they crash like glass globes into a thousand pieces. He takes more cherries out of the beaker. He asks if anyone wants to eat a cherry. There are no volunteers; so he eats them himself, throwing them into his mouth as he might salted peanuts.

Note what he has done. He states that his gas is nonpoisonous and that he will prove it. He pours gas into the beaker, explaining what he is doing. Then he shows the cherries, explaining that he got the bottle at the A&P. He drops them in the gas. He takes some out, demonstrating that they are frozen solid. He takes out more cherries. He asks if anyone wants to eat a cherry. No one volunteers and he eats them himself, saying, "If that gas is poisonous, I'll be mighty dead, for these are good cherries."

In this demonstration he gives the audience time to understand what he is doing. If rushed, that demonstration might not make its point clearly.

With any stunts make sure that the audience can see what you are doing. In my demonstration of the pencil I have to hold it high so that the group can see it. You have seen men hold up something for you to see. You had to move or raise your head to see it. It would have been better if he had held the piece high enough so that you could see without moving. The audience will go to some trouble to see what you offer, but don't ask them to do too much.

Each movement in a stunt should be planned with the audience in mind. A demonstration that you do for one man or two or three might not be good for an audience of twenty or thirty. In giving a demonstration on a stage, you may have to stand at the side of your machine. What you do will be of no interest to the audience unless they can see it.

When you plan what you are to do, decide how you are going to do it. Will you point with your left hand or right, and how will you point? With the index finger? With the finger on top or on the bottom? You might try both in front of a mirror to see which will look best to the audience. Plan each part of your stunt in this way. If you school yourself in what you are to do, you will do it naturally and easily, and it will look easy to the audience. Watch a magician do his tricks. You can learn a lot from him in making everything look easy.

In performing a bit of action, keep the audience informed of what you are trying to do. Once when I was upon a stage I started to show a small booklet. As I held up the booklet, my hand was shaking. The audience could see that booklet shaking; so I stopped my description of the booklet and said, "Look at that hand shake." The line got a laugh, and the hand stopped shaking. That stunt was not planned. I could have ignored the shaking hand and gone on with my description of the booklet, but every listener was watching the shaking and losing my point about the booklet. When I showed the booklet, I told them that I was going to describe it to them. They were waiting for my description. The shaking hand got in the way of that description. I had to give the hand some attention to get it out of the way. The engineer with the frozen cherries told the audience what he was going to do. Some speakers say, "Here's what I am going to try to do. I'm not so sure that it will come off." His statement is to get your interest and build suspense. He knows how it will come off because he has planned and rehearsed it.

If the stunt is in the nature of a demonstration, give the reasons why things happen. You say, "When I gesture with my hands like this, I put more energy into what I say. I can't help it." You gesture with your hands and you prove what you say. You say, "When I speak louder than I need to for this hall, note how I seem to have more conviction." You speak the same line twice, once in the normal tone and then in a louder tone. The listeners get the point because you have given them a reason.

It helps if you hold attention where you want it. In my pencil demonstration I say, "Look at this eraser." All eyes are on that eraser. Surely they have seen erasers before, but I asked them to look at this one. It must be something special.

In any stunt, be sure that your explanation explains what you are trying to do. They may laugh at your antics, but if they don't get your point, your stunt has not helped advance your talk. The shaking hand incident gave the idea for an elaborate stunt that was used in a series of meetings. The speaker held up a small appliance covered with a velvet cloth. He told what it was. At this point his hand began to shake. He looked at the shaking hand, apologized to the audience for being a bit nervous, and said he would lean on the lectern as he talked. He laid the appliance, still in the velvet cover, on top of the lectern, and grasped the sides of the lectern with his hands. Immediately the lectern started to shake. It seemed as if the appliance might be shaken onto the floor. The speaker seemed to be upset by this and laid the appliance on a table beside the lectern. The lectern stopped shaking and the table started shaking. The audience started to laugh. Now the speaker took up the appliance and said, "Gentlemen, there is no holding this new appliance. It will shake the industry just as it has shaken my hand, as it has shaken this lectern, as it has shaken this table. It will shake salesmen out of their lethargy. They will have to talk about it, about its good points—it's so new, so different, it's got so many real talking points, shoppers will insist that they talk about it." With that he took off the velvet cover, showed his appliance, and asked, "What do you think? I say there is no holding it. Dealers won't be able to keep it in stock."

The stunt had to be done with mechanical gadgets but it put over the speaker's point.

Not long ago I saw W. B. (Bill) Power, advertising manager of Chevrolet, give a talk. Bill is an expert at this type of histrionics. Here are some stunts that he did in this one talk.

At the start he took off his coat to show that he wasn't such a big shot as the introduction stated.

He demonstrated how he kowtowed to the vice-presidents. He got down on his knees, clasped his hands above his head, and bowed low to the floor, saying, "Yes, Mr. Ajax, yes, Mr. Ajax." He did this a number of times, using different names. Then to show that he had somebody under his supervision who would do the same for him, he had a stooge come in and bow low to him in the same way, saying, "Yes, Mr. Power, yes, Mr. Power."

He took ten silver dollars and threw them out to the audience.

At one point he pretended he had forgotten his place.

He imitated a drunk on the street walking with one foot in the gutter.

He used dialect in a number of stories.

He got down on his knees to illustrate a story in which the man was praying.

He took a large paintbrush and got down on the floor as if he were painting the stage.

There may have been more of these stunts, but the list shows how far some speakers carry their dramatics. You know that you would like to hear a man give that talk. The men who heard it applauded for minutes. W. B. Power is an expert at it. He has spent years learning how to do these stunts. He is much in demand as a speaker, as you might well imagine. And does he get his story over? He does. He serves his message with dramatics, and the listeners receive the message and love it.

When you plan to give a demonstration, have everything ready. In the pencil demonstration I have the pencil on the table in front of me. If you are talking at a dinner, keep your eye on such objects, for the waiter might cart them away with the dishes. I had that happen to the deck of cards I mentioned earlier in this chapter. The audience laughs when I fumble trying to get that newspaper clipping out of the folder in the inside pocket of my coat, but they are laughing with me, not at me. They know it is a stunt. But they laugh because they have seen speakers fumble in just that way.

Have everything ready and you won't get any laughs except where you want them.

Any demonstration should be planned. To show what I mean, let's take a simple demonstration and work it out. Assume that we want to show how a story gets garbled by repeated tellings. You decide that you can illustrate the point by starting with a square sheet of paper. The square sheet is to represent our correct story. It is correct when the first man tells it to the second. But when the second tells it to the third, he misses some of it. Now the third tells it to the fourth. Again some of the story is missed. The fourth tells it to the fifth and again some of the story is lost.

To illustrate this idea in a speech, you hold up the square sheet of paper. As the second man tells the story to the third, you cut a corner off the paper. When the third tells it to the fourth, you cut off another corner. When the fourth tells it to the fifth, you cut off another corner. You should stop then because if you cut off the other square corner your sheet may be almost square again.

You can tear off these corners, or you can cut them off with a pair of scissors. If you resort to tearing, you will have an irregular-shaped sheet which may add to the effectiveness of the demonstration. If you use scissors, you might even mark the sheet lightly with a pencil to show where to cut.

The first decision, then, is: Will you cut or tear? You will cut. All right. Now, how much? Better cut a few sheets and make cuts of different sizes, to decide. Let's start with a sheet of business-size letter paper and cut it square. Now you have a sheet about 8½ inches square. When you cut off a corner about 2½ inches, it looks about right, doesn't it? Cut the other two corners off, make one about 3 inches and the other about 1½ inches. That makes the sheet more irregular.

This is a demonstration in which you use both hands. Hold the paper in the left hand and the scissors in the right. If you are left-handed, reverse the hands. Before you give this demonstration, you should stand in front of a mirror with your square of paper and scissors, and check to see how high you should hold your hands. Then try cutting as you watch. The paper makes your point. It is what you want the audience to see. Work out your procedure with that in mind. What are the procedures you have to plan?

You have to hold up the paper while you tell what you are going to show. The audience has to see that it is square.

You have to reach up with the scissors and clip off the first corner.

You have to turn the paper so that you have it in place for the second cut.

You have to make the second cut.

You have to hold up the paper again and show the result.

You have to move the paper to get it in position for the third cut.

You have to make the third cut.

You have to hold up the paper to show how it looks after the three cuts.

Quite a bit of mechanics, isn't there, when you note each step?

You plan each movement with the idea that the audience can see and understand what you are doing. Nothing has been said about what you say while you go through each of these steps. This can best be done while you are planning the stunt. Tell yourself that you are going to say this while you reach up with the scissors. Better still, write both down.

With your demonstration planned, the next step is to rehearse what you say and practice what you do. I have found that I can get an idea of how my demonstration will work when I show it to a small group. I call together three or four of the fellows at the office, and do the stunt just as I have worked it out. Then I ask for suggestions. I happen to have around me a number of men who do this kind of work, and their advice is helpful. Your trouble may be that you can't rely on the comments you get, but you will get some practice and you may get an idea or two for improvement. As you give the demonstration for the small group, you can watch the reactions to see if your idea is getting over. At the end of such testing sessions, I ask the group singly, "What do you think I was trying to get over?" Their answers tell me a lot.

You might try having one of the group do the stunt. Drill him in the script and in the mechanics, and let him do it while you look on. Watching him, you may get some ideas. He will do some parts better than you. You will see others that should be improved.

You can record your talk, play it back, and listen to it. When you do this, you will make changes that will improve what you say. Usually when you work out a script, you think it explains your idea. When you listen to that script spoken in your voice, you will be able to find some of its shortcomings.

In any rehearsal try to simulate the conditions under which you will do the stunt before an audience. Will you be up on a stage? Behind a speaker's table? How many rows of seats will there be? Try to do your rehearsing with the speaking assignment in mind.

In many of these stunts you will get laughs—and that laughter is dangerous. It is like strong drink; the more you get the more you want. That's why you have to do your stunts in moderation. A few might be fine; too many might cause the group to say, "Well, he put on a good show." In your speech the purpose of the stunt is to help you put over a point. If the stunt helps, fine; if not, the speech may be better without it. Most of the stunts you see are designed to liven up a talk or to add novelty to a meeting. Roy Bridges had the problem of explaining why a woman should have an electric clothes drier. The talk came at a time in the meeting when the audience had been listening to a long session of talking. Now, Roy had charts for the talk, and he had good material, but because of his place on the program he decided to put his talk in the form of a dramatic monologue. He put on an apron and a sunbonnet. He got a large clothesbasket, some clothespins, and some clothes. Then, as he talked to an imaginary neighbor, he hung his clothes on the line. He hung a piece of clothing and then a chart, stooping to get the pieces and the charts out of his basket. As he stooped and straightened, he bewailed the hard job of drying clothes this way. His appearance started the laughter. As he made each point in the brogue of an Irish washerwoman, the laughter built up. When he had finished, he received an ovation.

His histrionics were highly successful, but note that they were started by a need for that kind of thing. The skit was not put on for the laughs. The message it got over was its objective. One skit like that was about all the program could stand. Another skit like it would have been too much. You may say, "But, Hegarty, I have seen speakers do act after act, and they were good." That's true, I've seen that, too, but what was this speaker trying to do? And did he do it? If it was to entertain, and he entertained, his formula was all right. If it was to get his message over, how did the message come out?

In any demonstration you do, go all out. If you are supposed to be confused, don't be mildly confused. The stunt goes over better if you put your heart into it. Think of all the things you have seen a confused man do, and do them. Stop speaking, look distressed, repeat the last sentence again, fumble a bit with your notes, run your finger under your collar, mop your brow with your handkerchief, scratch your head, and look at the chairman as if he might help. Do all of these slowly so that each member of the group catches on.

You may feel foolish doing the acting, but don't let the audience know that you feel that way. Try to give a good performance. Throw yourself into it; give it all the energy you have. If you feel that you can't put your heart into it, discard the idea.

Here is your program for learning to add dramatic showmanship to your speaking skills:

1. Try a simple stunt in the next talk you do.
2. Try to develop four gestures to be used with your speeches.
3. If you are an experienced speaker, check to see what gestures you are using now.
4. If you see another speaker do a bit of play-acting, try the stunt yourself. It is not stealing; no doubt he got his idea from another.
5. Get variety in the type of things you do, in gestures, in acts, in pantomime.
6. Make sure that the audience can see and hear anything you do.
7. Don't rush a demonstration; take your time. The listener can follow only so fast.

8. Tell the listeners what you are going to do.
9. Give reasons for what you are doing; say, "I am placing this card in this box . . ."
10. Hold attention where you want it. Say, "I want you to watch this."
11. Explain what you are trying to show. Remember the engineer with the cherries?
12. Have everything ready when you start your stunt. Even the best speaker looks funny hunting for his properties.
13. Plan what you are going to do and what you are going to say. Get a clear mental picture of both.
14. Rehearse and practice. Try your stunt before a group; have one of the group do it while you watch; try recording the speaking part and then listen to it.

Dramatics are an important tool of all good speakers. It takes practice to become skillful, but if you learn to mix a bit of play-acting into your talks, audiences will like you better.

The Development of a Stunt

You have heard a speaker give a talk in which he did a stunt, got a laugh or two, and yet made his point. You might ask, "How does a speaker work up such stunts?" Most stunts call for a bit of planning. Let me describe how one of mine was worked up.

I had been asked to do a humorous talk at a meeting of the National Society of Sales Training Executives. The Society had the problem that faces every club and every association—meeting newly elected members, graciously bringing them into the group quickly, and making them feel at home.

To point up the problem, one of the newer members had been asked at the previous meeting to put on a skit which showed how difficult it was for a new member to make himself known to the older members. The skit got plenty of laughs, but underlying the laughs the skit had the serious purpose of pointing out that older members should do something to make the newer members feel at home.

Since the new member had given the first skit, the chairman felt that an older member might give a talk that would be an answer to it. The answer would be humorous—as humorous as the skit, if possible—but it would point up the fact that the older club members wanted to make the new members feel at home and were willing to do something about it.

In planning the talk, I decided to base it on a number of fictitious interviews with new members. I would tell a story of how I came to the meeting with the high resolve of checking on how I might be able to make the new members feel at home. Then, as I tried to be nice to the new member, he would push me around. Such interviews would be humorous to the group, for I would be telling stories in which I was the goat.

How many such interviews? I hit upon three, for the rule of "one, two, three" described in Chap. 6 applies in such speech construction. As a common pattern for these interviews I decided I would approach each new member in a friendly, helpful manner, and each would treat me roughly, even discourteously.

How would I know the new members? I thought I might tell how I saw a man standing in the hotel lobby looking lonely and forlorn. I assumed he was a new member; so I approached him.

I got a reception badge. I would have to explain that this was not official, that I had one left over from the Elks picnic back home. I would put this on my coat to show the listeners how I looked as I approached each new member.

While I was working up this talk, I saw a young man in a hotel lobby combing his hair. This is one of my pet peeves—young men combing their hair in public—and it gave me the idea of having one of the new members standing in the lobby of the hotel combing his hair. As I told about this fellow, I would demonstrate by combing my own hair. I thought it might be best to do this stunt with a giant comb.

In Harrisburg, Pennsylvania, on my way to the meeting, I stopped in a drugstore to buy the comb. I found that the store had a special that day and were selling four combs for twenty-five cents. Since I was meeting three new members in my talk, that gave me the idea of having each of the men combing his hair when I first saw him. I would make this my clue to recognition of the new members. I decided to state, "Whenever you see a man combing his hair in public, he is lonely." I thought that statement might be ridiculous enough to get a laugh. It was.

Now I had three men combing their hair when I approached them. How could that be done? First, I would have one man combing in the regular way. I'd have the second fellow combing his hair down into his eyes. Then I would have the third man waving his head with a flourish as he combed.

Since I had a number of combs in the bargain package, I decided to have the first man comb his hair with a small comb, the second with a comb that had a handle, and the third with the giant comb.

Now with method and props agreed on, I had to rehearse to see how I looked combing my hair. I wanted to look funny, even ridiculous. I rehearsed the three methods before a mirror. The first demonstration needed no flourish because the first time I combed my hair the audience would be taken by the novelty of it.

But when I combed my hair a second time, I needed a different approach. This time I was to comb my hair down toward my eyes. As I practiced this before a mirror, I decided I would look funnier if I wore a pair of dark shell-rimmed spectacles. With the spectacles and my hair down I looked like an owl. That, I figured, was good for a laugh, and it was.

For the third demonstration I decided to wave my head with a flourish as I ran the large comb through my hair. I worked out the motion in front of a mirror.

With the stunt worked out, I needed a script. Here was my plan for that.

First, I worked up an introduction. It referred to the skit put on by the new member at the previous meeting. It explained that while other people laughed uproariously at the antics of the new member trying to get acquainted, tears welled up in my eyes, rolled down my cheeks, and the taste of salt was on my lips. I explained that we were fine people, that we welcome new members, that we like them, but from what this new member said we weren't getting the idea over.

Now came the three interviews.

In the first interview I met a man who asked me what business I was in. I told him I was in the electric-appliance business. He told me that he had bought a gas refrigerator. I asked him if he was in the gas business. I asked him if he could get a bigger discount on a gas refrigerator than he could on an electric. He told me he couldn't. He bought the gas because he thought it was better. Since I am an electric-appliance man, this conversation got a laugh.

Next, he brought out the fact that he had heard of me some place. We finally settled that it was because I had written a book. He told me he had seen one of my books once. I asked if he owned one. He said he didn't. I asked if he had seen it in the library. He said he hadn't. Finally, he told me he had seen it in a secondhand bookstore.

The second interview was with a fellow who was there to meet the members, but with a purpose. His boss had sent him to sell the members a gadget his company made. The gadget was a visual prop, a little toy I could demonstrate.

I described how, as he talked, he demonstrated his gadget and tried to sell it to me.

The third interview was with a new member who kept asking who various members were. I told him and asked if he would like to meet them. He said that he didn't want to meet three of our most prominent members, all past presidents. I asked why. Then, when I asked him why he had come to the meeting, he told me he was searching for the evanescent. At this I acted dumb. I didn't know what he meant. Then he explained, "It is difficult to explain, Mr. Hegarty. I am searching for that tremulous sheen on the fleecy cloud, that dash of faded cobalt in the blue sky, that burst of magenta in the sunset—do you follow me, Mr. Hegarty?"

By this time I was struck dumb. I told the group that at this point I threw my reception badge away. I tossed it over my shoulder. Note how, with each interview, I became more confused. First, I had a fellow who kicked me in the teeth, next one who was trying to use the society, and third a fellow who had a screw loose. I had milked the subject dry.

Then I became serious and told the new members how we had set up a reception committee for them. How we wanted them to become a part of the society quickly. How we welcomed them.

As a part of the close I used my smile-and-frown routine described on page 119. This is a routine I have used many times and I know it will work. In it I try to get the audience to frown at me. An audience will not do this. I make the point, when I try to make them frown and they won't do it, that a man can't frown when he is trying to frown. Then I get the audience to smile at me and everybody smiles. I used it to show how friendly this group was. I used the smile-and-frown routine because it was tested and was sure fire. This is good technique. If you can develop a few such stunts, you will find many uses for them.

I then suggested that a new member walk up to any old member, introduce himself, and say, "I've heard a lot about you, Mr. Old Member."

When the old member asked, "Just what have you heard about me?" I suggested that the new member ask the old member if he would mind standing over by the desk in the corner of the lobby and join the new member in singing the NSSTE song. I told the new members that there was no NSSTE song, but the old member would not know it.

That shows how a stunt is developed. It sounds like work, doesn't it? But this talk was a knockout. It got the laughs but also it did exactly what the group wanted it to do.

12

Some Life in Your Language

The other night at the end of a speech, one of the listeners said to me, "I think he used 'guy' too much, don't you?"

The speaker had referred to the group as "you guys," to the characters in his stories as "guys." I felt he had used the term too much.

"I realize what he was trying to do," the critic went on. "He is a member of our club and he was trying to be informal."

When I speak, I probably use that same term too much. Too many of the people I meet in my stories are "guys." And there is little reason for it. The character in my story might be a man, a fellow, a chap, or a lad. Yesterday I heard a man say, "I pushed this lad through a plate-glass window." The "lad" gave some life to the statement. You get a picture of two young fellows horsing around, but if the man who admits the pushing is in his fifties, you get an entirely different picture.

When you speak of a man, you might refer to him as a man, an old bird, a brother, a big shot, or perhaps a gentleman and scholar. Such appellations liven your speech; they picture the individual; they characterize him. You hear a speaker call a character "a big baboon." What do you get out of that designation? I see a big, rough, hairy individual of low I.Q., probably uncooperative. That is a load for two words, isn't it? Most speakers would call our baboon friend a chap, and so he would remain—a chap without honor, without personality, without anything.

In conversation most of us have life in our language; we use words and expressions distinctly ours. But somehow when we get up to speak we lose some of that life. We try to be as formal as our business letters that say, "Your letter of even date was received and its contents noted." If you were talking to the man, you might say, "Charley, that letter of yours is a lulu. . . ." Perhaps you don't write letters in the outmoded manner of that first quotation. But the man who writes letters like that speaks like a human being. If you called Charley on the telephone, you might say, "Look, I just got your letter. . . ." That sounds natural, doesn't it? Nothing outstanding about it, but it would go all right in a speech.

I am not suggesting that you search for zestful language outside yourself; just use the best you have. Any expression that comes naturally to you is certain to be better than one you read out of a book. In a magazine you may see a line, "A road or two dropped into the valley." The words express the idea beautifully, but in a speech they would sound affected.

One way to add life to your language is to use better verbs. Most of us use the same ones over and over again, and dead ones, too—to be, to have, to say, assures, enables, allows, enhances, satisfies, guarantees. It is a group of once stout fellows that have been worked until they are tired. When you write, "The men were complaining," your statement is ordinary. When you say, "The men were screaming," you are more descriptive. You might write, "The men were bellyaching" or "The men were beefing" or "The men were yelling their heads off." There are four choices—all better than the original statement. Which would best fit your subject and your personality?

Let's say you have a line, "The boys were discussing the subject." One of my friends used that as "The boys were beating their gums." To the ones in the know, the second statement means the same as the first, but does the audience know? If you want to use a stronger word than discussing, you might say, "The brothers were arguing back and forth" or "The brothers were debating" or "The brothers were disputing." Now, none of these is an unusual word; any one of them would be understood.

One speaker says, "You can't force them to do it." Another says,

"You can't mandamus them." Good—but will the audience understand?

I heard one speaker say, "My attention began to yawn." I imagine that he got that out of a book somewhere, but it was a line that could be understood, and one that got a smile from the audience. I heard one speaker say, in describing Winston Churchill, "He was savaging the end of a cigar." I didn't quite get it when the speaker said it. The man next to me repeated it. It is a good line, isn't it? But I am afraid it doesn't belong in a speech. It is a bit too unusual. It presents a picture, but the word "savaging" goes so fast that the audience may not understand it.

The speaker is inclined to write, "The boss gave him a severe reprimand." Perhaps that should be, "The boss burned his pants off." Now "burned his pants" has more life, but how about "seared his pants off"? Stronger, isn't it? Note that none of these words are unusual; any audience will understand them.

Now come the adjectives. Adjectives are dangerous in a speech, for often the speaker loses the adjective or the noun it modifies. He gives one so much emphasis that the other is lost. Still, strong adjectives can give life to your speech. The politician says, "My youthful opponent," and makes the adjective mean "inexperienced."

Courses for the experienced salesmen who might resent going back to school are called "refresher" courses. The same course may be given to the cub salesman as "basic training." Who can object to taking refresher training? You can use adjectives to build up and to tear down, but it is best to use them sparingly. If you will read through the talks printed in the proceedings of the last annual meeting of your national association, you will find that the speakers used few adjectives. As a rule, adjectives don't speak well.

You can add strength by using some of the language of youth. Pick up some of the jargon of your children. Use it in place of something stuffy. The substitution will show you are alive, that you know the world is progressing. Once my younger son called me a "drip." The next week I used it in a speech. A man came up after the talk and asked, "Say, where did you get that word? My youngster called me one last week."

The other day I heard a speaker say, "That's how it should be—but definitely." Where did that come from? From one of his youngsters, I bet. Children use an expressive language. Don't overlook it. Use a bit of it when you can.

Slang offers another source of life. A speaker says, "We got out of there." He might say, "We beat it out of there." He could use ran, stumbled, staggered, zoomed. There are many words to express his meaning, and not all are slang, either. The man in the story may say, "Get out." It may be stronger when he says "Scram." The slang of your boyhood may not work at all. It may be outdated, but it can be modernized. In my talk "How to Run a Meeting" I have one sequence in which I describe the man who is called upon by the chairman to say a few words on a subject. I say, "Brother So-and-So has no knowledge of the subject; he has no interest in it and no enthusiasm for it. Yet, because he is called, he gets to his feet and says, 'Ladies and gentlemen. . . .' He ums and ahs, then ums and ahs some more, and he hasn't talked long before everybody in the room knows that he is up the creek without proper equipment." Now that little shift from the original line gets a flicker from the audience. That "up the creek" is old slang, but the little twist makes it good.

The sports pages offer much lively language. I heard a speaker say, "This fellow couldn't find right field in any ball park." You have heard of the fellow who couldn't get to first base, the one who had two strikes on him, his brother who fouled out, or the man who didn't get the hit-and-run signal. Those are all out of baseball. They are perhaps the safest jargon to use, for many in your audience will know baseball chatter. But there is colorful language in football, basketball, and golf. It is a language of action and thus it has the life you may need in your speech.

Much of the life in our language comes out of the comics. It is good speech material, too, for most of the words in those strips are one-syllable words.

Now for colloquialisms. They come in handy. The man with the Southern accent can call the waitress in his story "Sugah." That sounds great. Anyone with an accent should not worry so much about getting rid of the accent as about pronouncing the words plainly with the accent. In every part of this country there are colloquialisms. A speaker from that part of the country will use those expressions naturally, and they will add charm and life to his talk. If you are given to using some of that sectional, state, or neighborhood jargon, use it. It is natural to you and takes you out of the stuffed-shirt classification.

This zestful language is remembered. Many times a man who has heard me talk reminds me of an expression I used a number of years before. I, too, remember such expressions.

There was an old vaudeville act in which a husband and wife were arguing about the guests at dinner.

"Who was that big walrus that sat next to you?" the husband asked.

"He was no walrus. He was a fine gentleman," the woman replied.

"What do you mean, 'fine gentleman'?" the man retorted. "We had to throw him a fish to keep him quiet."

That "throw him a fish" line has stuck with me through the years. I don't remember much about the act, but I do remember that one line. I've used it again and again.

So put some life in your language. Here are the suggestions that have been covered.

1. Look for stronger verbs; verbs that picture action.
2. Remembering that adjectives may be lost in the shuffle, use them where they will help, but don't trust them too much.
3. Steal some of the language of youth—one of your youngster's favorites, or one from the neighbor's kids.
4. Don't pass up the slang of the day. It is live language. It can add sparkle.
5. Lift some of the choice expressions of the sports pages. The

huddle, shift, single wing—they all express action that makes live speech.

6. Don't be ashamed to let them know that you peek at the comics after the children have gone to bed. There is a lot of life in a medium that 80 per cent of the public reads.
7. Use the expressions from your neck of the woods if you do it naturally. They give the group a picture of you.
8. In your stories don't call all your characters by the same name. They are all "guys," yes, but some variety in the naming adds snap to the talk.

Back in high school the teacher always said, "make haste"; the Frenchwoman across the lots called to her youngsters, "toot sweet"; the coach yelled, "make it snappy"; the sergeant growled, "snap into it." All meant the same thing. It is a great thing, this language of ours. We can put life into it in so many ways.

But don't do it if it is not natural to you. If you can't use that kind of language in your daily life, don't put it on for this audience. They can spot it, and when they do, you are a phony and your cause is no better.

13

Getting the Audience into the Act

The master of ceremonies says, "Give the little girl a hand." Why do we rush to oblige? Because the girl is good? Why, she hasn't sung a note yet. We applaud because that brings us into the act.

We all like to get into the act. The good speaker knows this and gets his listeners in, to help him make a better talk. He gets them to ask questions, to raise their hands, to stand up, do some exercise, repeat a phrase after him, sing a song, shake hands, speak to the person in the next chair, or walk around the table. You have seen speakers do all these stunts. And it makes the talk better, doesn't it?

Let's say you get the chairman to stand up and hold up a sign for you. They know the chairman and are glad to see him put into your act. Get one of the group to write figures on a blackboard for you, and have another help you do a demonstration of your product. But you do not need to stop with one person. Put them all to work. An audience will do almost anything for you if you know how to manage. You can get them to stand up and stretch, to say something with you, to walk around tables, or to scramble for souvenirs you throw to them. Not long ago I saw a speaker get them to prove that they liked to get into the act. He threw out tin whistles. The group scrambled as if the whistles were ten-dollar gold pieces. When each listener had one, he asked one row to toot, then the next, and then the next, now this side, then that side. He awakened a sleepy audience; they had fun and helped him prove the point he was trying to make which was—everybody likes to get into the act.

You may say, "You're way beyond me now, Hegarty. I couldn't

do any of those things." But you can. With some planning and work you will find that you can. So let's discuss some of the tricks you use in getting the listeners to help you make a better talk.

As a stunt windup in my talk "How to Run a Meeting," I always have the group stand up, raise their hands above their heads, and wiggle their fingers. I use that stunt to show how a speech should be ended—in high.

Here is the way I handle it. I say to the group, "Now I'll show you how a talk should end. At this time I'd like you to look around the room at the people near you. Note the fatigue on their faces. Note the perspiration on the baldheads. Every man in the room looks his age at this minute. You're tired. You've been sitting here for forty minutes listening to me. You've been breathing second-hand air. The room is filled with smoke. You're dog-tired. Now I'm going to show you something. I want every one of you to stand up. That's it, stand there, please. Come on. Every one of you. All of you stand up, please. O.K., that's fine.

"Now, I want all of you to hold your hands above your head, like this. Get them up, everybody. Get them as high as you can reach. Reach for the ceiling. That's it. Now I want everybody to wiggle his fingers ten times with me. Come on now, while I count. One, two, three, four, five, six, seven, eight, nine, ten. That's right. Thank you—much. You did that well. All sit down, please. All of you.

"Now look at those faces around you. They are alive; they are full of life. The man who was old a minute ago is now young and gay. The perspiration has somehow disappeared from the baldheads. That's one way to end your talk in high. Mr. Chairman, I give your audience back to you relaxed and refreshed."

You can imagine the fun an audience gets out of a routine like that. They like it. It's a surprise ending, and when I give them back to the chairman they are ready to stand up and cheer.

Note two things about this routine. First, I tell them exactly what I want them to do. Second, I keep after them until every listener does what I want. Men tell me, "Ed, I can't get audiences to do such things for me. I have tried, but it doesn't work for me."

If you have had trouble getting audiences to take part, perhaps the explanation is in the two points mentioned. You have to explain, and you have to keep after them.

Perhaps you can't do a routine as elaborate as this in your talk. But try asking for a show of hands. Tell them exactly what you want. Say, "Hold up your hand, like this, high." Then hold your hand high.

No doubt, the simplest participation is getting questions from the audience. I have heard speakers ask, "Are there any questions before I go on to the next point?" Usually such a question gets no response. Why, I don't know. But I do know that listeners with scores of questions will sit in stony silence when such a question is asked.

Recently I heard a speaker ask for questions. The audience gave him the silent treatment. But he had been around. He said, "I'm glad to see you understand the plan. If you have no questions, I have some." He started asking questions and in a few minutes he had a lively question-and-answer session going.

A good question-and-answer period can be a high point in any talk. Many times I have heard listeners comment, "The talk did not impress me, but that question-and-answer period was great." Usually the good question-and-answer period is planned—planned as a high point.

Even the simplest form of audience participation must be done right. Let's say you want a show of hands on a question. The speaker should let the audience know that the show of hands is important. He should explain the following points:

He wants them to raise their right hands.
He wants them to reach high.
He wants them to do it now.
He wants everybody to take part.

If he asks, "How many like the blue—come on, let's see a show of hands," he gets a few hands, none very high. He gets no idea of the enthusiasm of the group for the blue, or the other colors either. Notice the next time you try to get a show of hands from an audience. When a few hands go up shoulder high, you say, "More of you must have an idea on this. Come on, everybody in favor raise their right hands—high—like this." You raise your hand to show what you want. Now you are getting a better showing but you are still not happy. Everybody is not taking part. So you say, "O.K., let's all put our hands down. Now, I am going to ask you to do it again. It's important that we get an accurate count. Come on, now, all of you. Everybody in favor put up your hand. Everybody—now." You raise your hand, and hands go up all over the room—high—like yours.

In my time I have induced audiences to do almost anything. In getting the group to stand and raise their hands, what did I do? Isn't this about it?

1. Explained exactly what I wanted them to do. (Look around; stand up; raise hands; wiggle fingers.)
2. Kept after them until they did it.
3. Led them as they did it; showed them how.
4. Refused to be satisfied with half efforts.
5. Thanked them for helping.
6. Complimented them on how well they took part.

The last two numbers, five and six, are more important when you have an individual or a small group take part, but note that I did both in this windup stunt.

When you want the audience to say something after you, you've got to tell them that you want everybody to join in and use the full volume of their voices. If you don't do that, they will mumble the words. If you want them to go all out, make sure they go all out.

In opening school sessions for wholesale salesmen, I use the "good morning" routine mentioned in Chap. 4. Since this is the start of the day and I want the students to take part in other sessions throughout the day, on the first morning I tell the group I will start each day by saying good morning to them. In response they are to say to me, "Good morning, Ed Hegarty." I say, "Now let's try that, understand what you are to do? I say, 'Good morning' to you. You say, 'Good morning, Ed Hegarty' to me. Get that? Now, let's try it. Good morning, everybody." They greet me, but since the idea is new, they do it in a halfhearted way. I say, "I am disappointed; that's not good at all. I know you can do better than that. As I look at you today with all these bright and shining faces, I'm sure that you can put enough pep into this to greet me as a leader in a conference like this should be greeted. So we are going to do that again. I'm going to ask you again to greet me. Good morning, everybody."

This time it is a little better, but I'm not satisfied with the second greeting and I say, "No, that's still not good enough. I know you can do better than that. This group looks too intelligent to mumble like that. This time I want you to do it right. I want you to wake up the people in the rooms next door, even down on the next floor or in offices down the hall. This time let's put everything you've got into it. Here goes. Let's do it right."

I do the greeting again and they follow me. This time I am satisfied. Note the routine: first they do it poorly, then a little better, and then well.

On this routine I purposely do not ask them to shout the greeting the first time they do it. If they did shout, there would be little to complain about. But if you want a group to shout, tell them you do.

Men who have been to this school tell others, "He makes us say 'Good morning' to him. And he is mighty particular about how we say it." Through such small things audiences remember you.

When I talk before a dinner meeting, I always move the men at the head table out from behind me. Men all over the country say, "He's the fellow who moves the head table out from behind him." This is a staged bit. Beforehand, I tell the men at the head table, "After I have talked a few minutes I'll ask you men to take your chairs and move out front. I want you to do it, but don't look happy about it; look as if you don't like the idea."

"Can I grumble?" someone usually asks.

"That's the idea," I say.

This bit of audience participation goes over great with the audience.

When I ask the men to move, usually someone says, "I'll move before you are introduced."

I say, "No, wait until I ask you, please." If the group moves before I request it, I have no stunt.

Arranging for cooperation beforehand can work in small bits, too—on questions, on a show of hands, on any other stunt.

Suppose you ask a few men to raise their hands when you ask them. Wouldn't that help in getting the group to raise their hands? When you want a man to help in a demonstration, arrange with him beforehand.

You have seen the little fellow on the street selling fountain pens. He asks, "Who wants the first one?" A man steps up, hands over his dollar, and takes the pen. You may feel that first purchaser is an associate, but you know all the others who follow are not.

Follow this plan when you want help in a demonstration: Arrange for the help beforehand; then, when you need the help, ask, "Who will help me demonstrate the point?" You pause and add, "How about you?" Point at the man who has agreed to help. The group urges the man you selected to give you a lift.

When the group sees one of its number do a demonstration with you, they say, "If he can do it, I can." The use of the stooge helps prove your point.

When you have the audience do a stunt, you are like the cheerleader in front of the stands. You have to lead—do the stunt yourself and get them to help you.

In my talk on "The Language of Selling" I use a routine I claim will improve the English of the audience 50 per cent. All they need to do is to watch how they say three little words. Then I show a chart which reads:

GET

ING

YOU

YES

I then say, "There are four words—or rather three words and one ending. If you would learn to pronounce each of those words properly each time you speak them, you would improve your speech. Let's talk about them.

"How do you pronounce that first word? Come on, now, somebody call out the correct pronunciation. A little louder, please."

A voice from the audience calls, "Get."

I say, "I am glad to hear that. It's good to know that some of you do know how to say the word. But how many of you say 'Get'?"

At that they smile. They know what I am after. In the Middle West almost everybody says "Git." Then I have the group repeat the word correctly. I say, "When I count three I want all of you to say 'Get' three times, like this: get—get—get. O.K., all ready now—one, two, three: get—get—get."

I then say, "How do we pronounce that ending? Let's say we want to say, 'I am going.' How do we say that?"

The audience has the point now. A number call out, "Goin'." I then have the group say, "I am going." I say, "When I count three, I want all of you to say, 'I am going' three times—one, two, three: I am going—I am going—I am going."

I go through the same routine with the other words, and then say, "Well, now, that's fine. Now let's put those words in a sentence. What can we say with them? Ah, here's one—'Yes, you get going.' That's good, isn't it?

" 'Yes, you get going.' Get it? Now I will count three, then you say it three times—one, two, three: Yes, you get going—Yes, you get going—Yes, you get going.

"Say, we've got something here. Let's do that like the old locomotive college cheer. Come on now. I'll count three, we'll start saying it slow, then we'll increase speed with each saying, and we'll have a locomotive yell, and our English lesson, too. O.K., now everybody ready—one, two, three: 'Yes, you get going, yes, you get going, yes, you get going, yes, you get going, yes, you get going—*stop*."

That routine comes at a point in the speech where I need some life. I have been talking rather seriously, quoting some facts about speaking English, and I am losing the attention of some of the group. At that point I spring the routine. As you look it over, you see that it could be cut much shorter. You might eliminate that locomotive stunt at the end. But I can say this—used completely, just as it is explained, it goes over beautifully.

There is another point to note in this routine. I ask the group to say "yes" three times. The word "yes" alone would go too fast. When I get them to say, "Yes, yes, yes," and time them by raising and lowering my hands, the words are given enough time.

I say that a speaker can get an audience to do anything—but I have never been able to get an audience to frown at me. I have tried it scores of times in a part of a speech that plays up the value of a smile. I make the point that it takes fourteen facial muscles to frown, only five muscles to smile. To prove that, I ask the audience to frown at me. I ask them to imagine that I am the boss, the landlord, the mother-in-law, a Democrat or Republican, someone they don't like. I plead and I cajole, but they sit there grinning at me. I work at this as hard as I work at any other audience participation stunt, but I can't get a frown. Perhaps a psychologist can tell you why. I can't, but I have tried it and I know it cannot be done.

When I ask that same audience to smile, I get the response I want. After trying this stunt a number of times, I changed the routine. I still try to get the group to frown. But I use their inability to frown to prove the point that it is difficult to frown when you are thinking about what you are doing, easy to smile.

There may be times when you want the audience to answer a question for you. You may ask them for an answer that seems quite obvious, and still you won't get it. At such times it might be well to indicate that you heard the right answer. No matter what question you ask, you'll get some answer, but it may not be the one you want. When you get these answers, you can pretend that you heard the one you wanted and say, "That's right," and then state the one you wanted.

I have a spot like that in one of my speeches. The chart which I use reads "Use Your Big Mouth."

When I show this chart, I talk for a while, and then I ask, "What's the first rule any salesman should learn about using his big mouth?" The answer I am after is, "Keep it shut."

Usually this answer comes almost immediately. Other times, the audience gives me all sorts of answers. I let this go on for a while, then I pretend that I have heard the right answer and I say, "Yes, that's right—keep it shut."

Whenever you ask members of an audience to take part, don't make fun of your helper, no matter how awkward or dumb he seems to be. He probably feels bad enough about it, anyway. Remember, you are prepared. He isn't prepared and you have a big advantage.

Many times I have wondered about the quiz masters or stunt masters on the radio. Frequently they make fun of participants, and I have wondered why the participant did not sock the M.C. so lacking in good taste. But you have good taste; so never make fun of anyone who takes part in your program.

By this time you are probably saying, "Well, I couldn't get an audience to do anything, or even one member of the audience to do anything, so don't worry about my making fun." Yes, getting the group or any of its members to take part comes first. But don't reject it as a speech device until you have tried it.

Not long ago I was working with a fellow in a series of meetings, and in one place he did a demonstration of a machine that couldn't be seen by the audience. I suggested that he have somebody from the audience help him. "You explain and he will operate the machine according to your directions," I advised. "I couldn't do a thing like that," the man said. "It would embarrass me."

If I had asked him to wear a funny hat, do a dance, stand on his head, or do any elaborate comedy stunt, I could have understood his reaction. But this seemed simple to me. After a little selling I got him to try it. His first attempt went off well. When it was over, he admitted, "Well, that wasn't difficult at all."

And it isn't difficult, even though you are thinking that audience participation is not for you. Next time you give a talk, have the audience do something for you. Ask for a show of hands; ask them to repeat something after you; ask each to look at his watch.

If you find these simple things work, go on to more elaborate stunts. Remember, an audience is sitting there listening to you. They feel it's your show. If you give them a part in the show, they are more inclined to like you and to feel that your show is better.

There is one caution—you can do too much. In one forty-minute talk I tried eight stunts. A listener said to me afterward, "I never saw so much audience participation." I said, "I don't think you will again." I believe that four or six would have been better for that talk—one every seven or ten minutes.

Now let's go over these suggestions again:

1. When you want audience participation, explain what you want the audience to do.
2. When you make such a request, keep after the group until they do it.
3. Never be satisfied with half efforts. Make them give and give.
4. Never make fun of a participant.
5. Thank any individuals for the help you get. Ask the others to applaud the helper.
6. Compliment any participant on how he does the stunt you have asked him to do.
7. Explain what you want fully. If you want them to raise their hands, tell them which hand, and how high.
8. Don't do any audience participation stunt too fast. Drag it out to heighten the effect.
9. Remember that you may have to coax or cajole the group into doing what you want. They want to take part, but they are not sure that everybody will join in.
10. When you want questions or testimonials, it is a good idea to arrange for them beforehand. Arrange for enough questions so that the questioning is sure to start.
11. You can also arrange for help you want from members of the audience. Some briefing or rehearsing might help.

12. Don't use too much audience participation; a little helps.
13. Don't assume that you can't get audience participation because you have not tried for it. You can if you are willing to work for it.

Next time you see a song leader lead a group in song, watch his technique. You can learn from him. Also note how everybody seems to enjoy helping out. If they enjoy taking part, why not give them some fun along with your sage advice? Remember, there is no truer statement than, "Everybody wants to get into the act."

14

Spacing the High Points

Once a fellow who was to speak on a program with me tossed some typewritten sheets to me. "Here's the script for my talk," he said.

I started through the pages. About the middle of the third page there was a note, "Shoot gun."

"What does that mean?" I asked.

"I'll shoot a gun at that point," he explained. "That oughta wake them up."

The man had an idea that might be applied to most speeches. Why do you need this relief? Well, old man fatigue is working against you. If the listener were at home in his easy chair listening to the radio or watching TV, he could drop off into a doze whenever he felt the urge. At home it would make no difference to anybody.

But as one of your audience, you don't want him to go to sleep. And the cards are stacked against you. The room is probably warmer than the one at home, the air is stuffier and decidedly secondhand, he doesn't know what to expect from you, and he had such a good nap during the speech at the last meeting. Yes, it might be a good idea to have that six gun ready and loaded.

Of course you can't carry a gun, a siren, or a whistle around with you to wake up listeners, but you can use certain speech elements to produce the same effect. A high point might be:

A story that gets a big laugh
An unusual stunt—taking off your tie, putting on a lady's hat
A bit of audience participation

A dramatic bit in which you act out a point
An unusual exhibit or property—the big sign drops from the ceiling
A startling bit of news, an unveiling
A good ending

These are some of the elements you have to work with. Your problem is to space these high points. After I had finished a speech some time ago, a friend said, "Ed, you had something happening all the time." I thought that a fine compliment, for I had planned it that way.

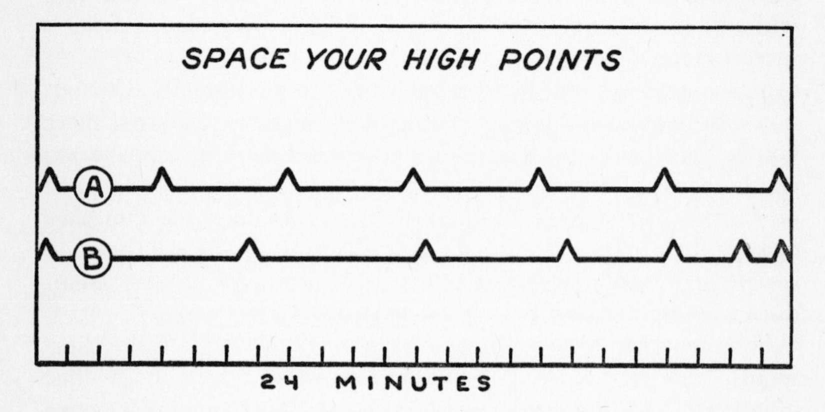

There are two ways you can do it. The diagram above shows how. Let's say line *A* is the flow of your speech and the bumps in the line are high points. In this arrangement the high points are evenly spaced. This is all right. You go so long, and then you "shoot a gun." In line *B* a different organization is shown. High points come faster as the speech goes on, a bit farther apart at the start, but closer together as you near the end. This is on the assumption that the audience is fresh when you start. A high point at the start gets you off; after a period of four minutes you hit them with your second point; three minutes later comes your third, in two and a half minutes your fourth, in two minutes your fifth, then one after one and a half minutes, and then one every minute until you close. Under this plan you shoot that gun oftener as they get drowsier. (The spacing times given above are merely to make the idea clear.)

How many high points do you need in a speech? One of my friends answers this with "Enough to keep the audience awake." If you plan your speech in units, I would advise, "Put at least one in every unit." If a unit is long, you may need more than one.

Could all the high points be stories that get laughs? Many good speeches are built on that plan, but a mixture is usually better. If you are a good storyteller, you might rely on the story alone. But even so, a stunt now and then, or a bit of audience participation, will add to the effectiveness of your talk. Variety helps make a speech better.

Many speeches will have enough high points but the distribution will be faulty. The high points will be at the start, and there will be long, dull stretches in the body of the speech. Some speakers think, "I'll wake them up at the start, and then I'll go to work on them." This type of thinking overlooks the fact that you have to keep them awake all through the speech. If you notice the good speakers, just about the time you seem to lose interest they introduce a high point, and you are on the band wagon again.

Usually, when you organize a speech, you say, "I'll make these points." To get your high points spaced right, why not list your points and then, opposite each one, make a note of how you are going to make a high point as you cover the point. Your list of points might look like this:

Point one. Show a page out of a newspaper that helps make the point.
Point two. Tell a story that gets a laugh but helps make the point.
Point three. A dramatic bit, in which you act out the point.
Point four. A bit of audience participation.

By listing the high points in your subject, you make certain that you have high points; and if each is planned to help emphasize one point, you will not have them bunched.

You may say, "Now you are getting too technical." This *is* technical, but you have to study the technique of speaking if you are to be a good speaker. Norman Vincent Peale, one of the best speakers I ever heard, asked me, "What do you consider your best story in that talk?" He had just heard me do my talk "How to Run a Sales Meeting."

"The Indian story," I replied.

"I remember it," he said. "Will you tell it to me again?"

I would and I did. Then I asked him to tell me his favorite story. Both of these stories were high points in our speeches; both got big laughs; both helped us make points.

I am telling this story to illustrate what speakers talk about when they get together. The good ones talk technique; they study speaking. If you make any part of your living by speaking, it will pay you to study these technical angles.

Can a speaker have too many high points? I believe this is possible. I have seen speakers use too many properties, too many demonstrations, too many stunts, and the result was confusing to the listeners. This is common in product presentations where the speaker has an elaborate demonstration of each feature of the product.

Let's now consider how almost any element of your speech can be built into a high point. You plan a demonstration of an electric range. You want to show how large the oven is. You want to build this demonstration into a high point. You have been opening the door of that oven and saying, "This oven is large. It is large enough to take the largest roaster pan that you can find in any home in this town. I'll tell you what I'll do. If any of you people in this room can bring me a roasting pan that will not go into this oven, I will give you five dollars cash. Just a minute." (You dig out your wallet, take out a five-dollar bill, and hold it up for all to see.) "There's a five-dollar bill. I'll give it to anybody who, before tomorrow evening, brings me a roasting pan that I can't get into that oven."

That would make a high point, wouldn't it? Let's say you have been using it for some time and it has not been going over as well as you would like. Why not build it up with a bit of audience participation? Let's say that when you offer your five dollars, a voice from the audience calls out, "Here's one right here."

You ask, "Is it a big one?"

The voice replies, "Bigger than that oven."

"All right, bring it up," you say.

The man brings up his roasting pan. You measure it. You ask some questions. After the audience knows the size of the pan, you try to put it in the oven. Of course you succeed, but you have made a higher point out of the five-dollar offer.

You can always make a high point with an anecdote. If you have one that gets a mild laugh, you may need one that gets a better laugh. Can you find better stories? I believe you can. Sometimes a member of the audience will give one to you. Recently, after a speech in which I advised the use of small words, a listener told me, "I have a story that you can use to illustrate that point."

"Good, let's hear it," I proposed. Here it is:

A gentleman of the cloth, who never used a small word where three or four large ones would do, arrived in a Southern town. At the railroad station he got into a taxi and said to the Negro boy driving, "On the way to the hotel stop at a haberdashery."

The boy said, "Yessuh, I'd be glad to."

When they stopped at a traffic light, the boy asked, "What's that place you say you wanta stop, suh?"

"A haberdashery."

"Yes, suh."

They went one more block and again the boy asked, "Did you say haberdashery, boss?"

"That's right, haberdashery."

Within a block of the hotel the boy again looked back. "Boss, you're going to have to tell me plain. What is it you want—liquor or women?"

This story was better than the one I was using. I substituted it and made a high point where I needed it. Yes, it is usually possible to get better stories.

Perhaps you have a story now that makes your point so well that you do not want to give it up. Can you build up that story? In Chaps. 5 and 6 I gave some suggestions for strengthening stories. Try these on the story you have, and see if you can't make it a better story.

Since I write my talks in units, I use this plan for spacing high points:

1. A high point for the start
2. A high point for each unit; if the unit is long, a high point in each part of the unit
3. A high point at the end

Look for these high points in the speeches you hear. Does the speaker space them right? If too many are in one part of the speech, is the remainder of the speech dull by comparison? Listen to what the speaker says, but note his technique, too.

Here again are these suggestions for high points:

1. You need high points at intervals to keep the attention of your audience.
2. Your high points should be spaced through the speech so that they hold interest from start to finish.
3. Any one of the speech elements can be built into a high point —story, news, stunt, acting, audience participation, exhibit, or a good ending.
4. You should have enough high points to keep the group awake all through your talk.
5. You can have so many high points that you confuse the audience.
6. Any speech device can be built up into a high point; anything you can do, you can do better.
7. Try for a high point at the start of your speech, one at the end, and one at least in each unit.
8. Experience will show where you need high points. Do a talk once and you will find parts that could stand a boom from the six gun.

This chapter started with a story about shooting a gun. Let it end on the same theme. Realize that you need the effect of that big boom again and again throughout your speech. Shoot that gun three times at the start, and I may go to sleep on you before you end. Shoot it three times at the end, and you awaken me for the next speaker. Shoot it every two minutes during the talk, and you will have me with you from beginning to end.

15

Build up to the End

What do you know about the curve of audience interest in a speech?

The other noon we came out of a meeting of a service club. The man with me said, "I didn't think this speaker was going to be so hot when he started, but as he got going he sure held attention."

The speaker knew about the curve of audience interest; he knew that it should go up and up from the start. It is what you want your speech to do—to get them at the start and to hold them tighter, tighter, tighter as you go on. A speech should build up. It should start low and build up to a high point.

My plan is to organize the end of a speech first. That gives me a good ending. I put so much in the ending that there is plenty of room for the earlier material to build up. Often a speaker uses his best material first, then brings on the lesser points, and when he approaches the end he is giving them ums and ahs. Some speech instructors advise you to kindle interest in your first sentence. That may be fine for the two- or three-minute speeches of the speaking classes. But haven't you heard this comment, "He started great, but he didn't live up to his opening"?

As has been said before, when you start with an audience it is usually fresh. It looks at you, hoping for the best but with its fingers crossed. Your job is to hold its interest from that start until you finish. One sure way to do that is to keep getting better as you go along.

I like to work on what I call the GBB formula. That means

Good: Better: Best.

I try to apply this order to units, stories, stunts, properties—the good unit first, the better one next, and the best one last. When you think of this order in your speech, you are not likely to put all your best material first.

One of my friends starts all his speeches with a series of stories. His stories build up. His first is weak, his next stronger, his next stronger yet, and so on. I have watched this man work, and I can say that this plan is good for a start. "It gets me off swell, Ed," he says, "but too often I am never able to get them back to the pitch I reached on the last story."

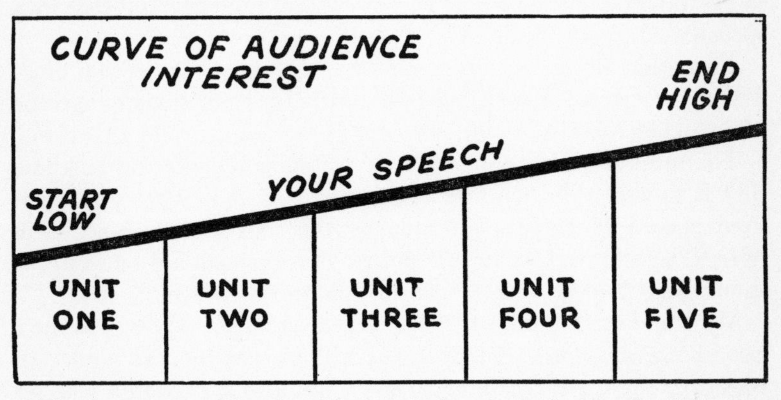

Not long ago a friend and I attended a musical comedy. After we had sat through ten minutes of the first act, my friend said, "This is a waste of time."

I agreed that it was. Then within a minute the tempo began to pick up, action increased, and laughs came faster. At the end of the first act, the audience was ready to stand up and cheer. Here, I thought, was the pattern for a good talk—start slowly and build up.

Suppose you have an anecdote about an ordinary character in each unit of your speech. Would it harm the speech too much if you switched the anecdotes around so you could use the good one first, the better one next, and the best one last? You may not always be able to do this, for one story may be so pertinent to the point made by the unit that it belongs in that unit. But if you are trying for this build-up effect, it would be a shame to waste the best story in the first unit, wouldn't it?

I have suggested that you start low. This does not mean that the start should be so low that the listeners will feel sorry for you. Start as well as you can, but organize so that what comes later is better. You may say, "What about logical order?" Remember this, listeners do not hang on every word, checking to see if you have marshaled your points in logical order. You alone will know that. Perhaps not one of the listeners will have put the time and effort you have on this subject. The other day one of my associates, who had just finished making a good talk, said, "I covered all my points, but I did not get them in logical order."

"Don't worry about that," I advised. "Nobody knows the order you should have used, nobody but you. If you don't tell, nobody will suspect."

For some reason speakers seem to think that an audience is analyzing what the speaker says more closely than it does. Some few listeners in a group may analyze what you say, but most of them just listen, and not too attentively at that.

The build-up can also be arranged within a speech unit. The formula given for a speech unit on page 13 is:

1. A statement of the premise
2. A quotation from an ancient
3. A quotation from a poet
4. One from the Bible
5. An anecdote about a famous character
6. The same about an ordinary character
7. A second statement of your premise

As you glance at that formula, you see that it is in logical order. It goes from past to present. To work out the build-up in a unit that had all these elements, you might start with those statements of the premise. Make the second statement stronger than the first. Perhaps your quotation from the ancient might be stronger than the one from the Bible. All right, reverse the order. The story about the famous character might be stronger than the one about the bartender and the blonde in the Elite Bar and Grill. Put the best one last and you have a unit that builds up. You may not go from past to present, but you build up. If one of the earlier elements in a unit is so strong that the remainder of the unit can't be built up, consider eliminating the element that is too strong. You may have a better speech if you cut it out altogether.

Follow this idea in using all your material. Let's say you have a new model of your product at an exceptionally low price. You are to present this model to a group of salesmen who will sell it. You feel that your price story is your big point, but you have new color, new styling, new design, and two new features in addition to the new price. Price is the big feature; therefore to build up, you would present your story in this order:

The color
The styling
The new design
The two new features
The price

In making this list, I assume that the order is the order of importance. I would cover the good feature first, the better one next. Let the story build up from start to finish.

Your stunts should build up in the same way. In Chap. 13 we talked about shooting a gun. Well, don't shoot a cannon in the first unit and a cap pistol in the last. Remember the man in the vaudeville act who came out first with a small hat, changed to a larger one, and kept doing similar changes for fifteen minutes until he had a hat he couldn't lift. That act was planned with the idea of building up. It is the GBB formula in action. Joe Cook would imitate one Hawaiian, then he would imitate two Hawaiians, and then he would talk about imitating three Hawaiians, but he would never do it. It was build-up, the kind you need.

The same thought should be given to the exhibits you use. If you start your speech waving a small American flag, wind up by waving a huge one. The man who gives a chart talk may not be able to get this build-up in size, but he doesn't have to have a letdown, either. He could make his later charts more interesting than the first. He might use plain type on the earlier charts, and then cartoons on the later ones. Some such device could carry out the idea. Not long ago I saw a speaker use a set of cartoon charts, and each succeeding one seemed sillier than the first. He used the device to get laughs, and he succeeded. The same effect is good in the properties or speaking aids you use: small ones first, larger ones later, largest ones last.

Audience participation should be thought of in the same way. Ask for a show of hands first, then get the audience to stand up, and then get them to say something after you. It is easier to get them to do the simple things first. After they start to help, they do the more complicated stunts easily. But the build-up helps. Never ask a group to do the tough stunt first; do the easy one first.

This technique of the build-up in speechmaking is little understood. Recently a man gave me a verbal outline of a speech he was to make. When he had finished, I suggested a change in the order. "That's a good idea," he commented. "It will put the more important parts last."

The man knew what I meant when I made the suggestion, but he had not planned to cover the points in the order that would give him the most effective build-up.

Watch that you don't expend all your energy in the first part of the speech. Save some of it for the home stretch. Not long ago I spoke to a most disorganized meeting. The chairman would not give the group a recess, and when I was introduced, at least a quarter of the audience started to leave the room. I took the introduction and suggested the recess. In ten minutes most of the audience was back, but they all sat in the rear seats. I took on the job of moving them into the front seats. They were reluctant, and it took quite a bit of my energy to get them seated as I wanted them. Finally, I started my talk. The chairman should have seated the audience and saved me the trouble. I am sure that the talk I gave that day was not up to my best. I had worn myself out seating the group.

A speaker should hold back that reserve energy to throw into the last part of his talk. He should put a bit more fire into his voice, his gestures, and his movement. His expenditure of energy will help keep the group awake. I have said that the audience is fresh when you start. Remember, you are fresh, too, and if you tire yourself out in the first few minutes, you may be sagging as you come into the stretch. If you don't go all out at the start, if you hold back some of your energy, you have a better chance of coming into the stretch steaming up the listeners by your enthusiasm.

What you want in any speech is a building-up, up, up, and up. You start on a low point—good, mind you, but not your best—and then you start to climb. As you tear into your finish, you are getting better. Better stories, better stunts, better audience participation, bigger news, larger props or exhibits—that's the idea. You may not be able to follow this plan all through your speech but you can try. And because you try for this effect, and consider ways and means to attain it, your speech will be better.

Now let's consider these points again:

1. Check the curve of audience interest. Does it build up?
2. Try for a build-up in the importance of the points you make—minor points first, major points last.
3. See what you can do about the GBB formula.
4. Look for a build-up within each unit.
5. Arrange the units so that you follow the GBB formula.
6. Check the material used throughout the speech—the anecdotes, stunts, dramatic bits, data, news, audience participapation, and exhibits. Do they get bigger and better as you go along?

When you think of this build-up, let your memory go back to the pin-ball machine addict in the movie. In every scene he is playing that pin-ball machine, and always losing. Each time he goes away for more change, he seems sadder, more forlorn than the time before. Then his patience is rewarded. On his last ball on his last nickel, all the lights light up, a music box inside the contraption plays "The Star Spangled Banner," and, as the addict stands at salute, the machine explodes.

Would that more speakers could get that kind of build-up into their speeches. It will pay you to try.

16

Try to End in High

The young man asked the experienced speaker, "What is the best advice you can give about making a speech?"

The elder hesitated not at all. "Get a good ending," he said.

And that is sound advice. Once I worked with a fellow who said, "When I have a good ending, I can always stop. Let's say the hall catches fire. I go into that ending, and I get out before the fire engines arrive." It would pay most speakers to adopt this idea.

You have heard the speaker who comes to the right place to close and talks right past it. He comes to another natural terminus and breezes right on. Then another and another. If he had stopped at any one of those places, he would have made a good speech, but he didn't stop.

If you are going to be a good speaker, learn how to end well. You have many devices you can use: you can sum up, assign the job, repeat a three-step formula, repeat your premise, tell a story, recite a poem, do a stunt, or get audience participation. Here are some examples of how these devices have been used.

Let's say you want to sum up. Here is how I do it in my speech "How to Get Better." My plan for training is expressed on one of the charts: "Use Your Eyes, Ears, Big Mouth, and Practice." This chart is shown when I give the formula early in the talk. Then close to the end of the talk I ask, "Remember that plan?" and I show another chart with the identical wording. I have given the audience a plan, I have talked about each step of the plan, and then I sum up by stating the plan again.

Let's say you are asking for contributions for the Community Chest. You say, "Here's why you should give: first, this; second, this; third, this." The three-point ending is good. The audience can remember three points. If you give them more, you may confuse them.

Any audience likes this type of orderly ending. They feel that you have given them a plan. You hear a speaker make a plea for a cause. He covers all the points but somehow he doesn't seem to make much of an impression. The fellow next to you asks, "What does he want us to do?"

Might that be because he has not summed up? Advice scattered through a speech may be lost. Sum up that same advice at the end of the talk, and your listeners will know what you want them to do.

Your ending can assign the job. You want these workers to do something. All right, give them a plan of work in your ending. You say, "You call on the three men named on these cards. You ask this question. You write the answers on the reverse side of the card." That is clear, isn't it? Could any worker misunderstand those directions?

Your ending can repeat the premise. Let's say your premise was, "It Pays to Smile." Here is one I use in a little talk I do on that subject. "Yes, a smile pays. It paid Charlie Schwab. It pays the salesperson in the store. It pays the man who owns the store. And it will pay you. Try it tomorrow, please, in the morning when you first get up. Smile at that fellow in the mirror. Smile at the girl who gets your breakfast. Smile at the first ten people you meet. You will make the day brighter for all of them, and for you, too. Yes, it pays to smile."

That ending is a summing-up of what I said. It reminds the listeners of the examples I used and it restates the premise.

The formula ending is one of the most popular. I like the one, two, three type of ending: first, do this; second, do this; third, do this. A few months ago I gave a speech on public speaking before a speaking club. To illustrate how the formula ending works, I took three of the speeches I heard that night and worked out a formula ending for each.

One man talked about the condition of the city streets. He wanted the group to get after the city fathers and do something about it. Most of his listeners agreed that something should be done. He could have wound up in this way.

"If you want these streets repaired, here is a plan. Tonight, when you go home, sit down and write a letter to your councilman. Better still, tomorrow telephone him. Then get the first two men you meet tomorrow to do the same. Get enough telephone calls made and enough letters written, and we'll get those streets fixed. All you do is these two things:

"First, write or telephone your councilman.

"Second, get two of your friends to do the same."

A second man talked about the history of the city. He was a newcomer to the town, and his talk was a rambling story of how the city came into being and how it had grown. His ending was a casual report on the fun he had digging out the material for the talk. He could have made his ending into a formula thus:

"I got a great kick out of getting the information for this talk. Most of it came out of a stone building over on Third Street, the public library. I imagine that some of you have never been through those doors. I hadn't before I started out to get the information for this talk. Now I have developed an interest in the history of this town. I am thinking about enlarging my interest to the county and then to the state. So I say to you, if you are looking for a new interest, select a subject and go see what you can find in the library about it. Then, here is a plan that will open up new worlds for you:

"First, take the new interest to the library, and talk to the attendants there.

"Second, get the books that are available, and read them.

"Third, make the information yours by putting it into a speech like the one I did tonight."

A third man spoke about how the tone of your voice affects the people around you. His was pretty much an acting job as he played the parts of the persons he imitated. The talk was a demonstration of his ability to do such a talk, and working out a formula ending; for it was not too easy. But here was the attempt:

First, your voice can help you get along with people.

Second, watch it when you speak to others.

Third, use it right and you can make friends; use it carelessly, and you will turn people from you.

When you are stuck for an ending, use the three-step formula. It is good for any extemporaneous speech. Let's say the chairman calls on you for a few words on a subject to which you have given not the slightest thought. When placed in such a spot, don't worry at all about the body of your speech. Think of three things the club should do about it and build an ending around them. You will usually feel a bit foolish when you start to talk on a subject on which you are blissfully ignorant, but the ending will give you confidence. You say, "Gentlemen, this is my program. First, we should do this; second, this; and third, this." When you sit down, you won't have to wait for the applause.

Thousands of speakers have been thrown into this situation, and most of them have done poorly. When they finish, the audience asks, "Why was this guy asked to speak anyway?" But the speaker who knew how to end a speech earned this comment and got it, "This fellow always has ideas." Neither had ideas, but one had an ending that sounded like a plan. So make the formula ending one of your speaking skills.

Another effective ending not too difficult to learn is the bit of poetry that tells the group you are finished. Select a piece, learn it, and recite it as your ending. You have a wide field of selection. There are the speakers' friends Kipling, Service, Harte, or Guest; the typical American poems such as "The Face on the Barroom Floor" and "Casey at the Bat"; and the native poetry of the part of the country in which you originated.

With the longer pieces you have to memorize the words and rehearse. This is work. The short piece may tell you whether or not you are cut out for poetry. The other night I heard a speaker use this:

Ten minutes back,
I stood up and begun,
Now that I've spoken,
I'll sit down, I'm done.

That doesn't sound like much, does it? But the man made it an effective ending. It did one job well—it told the listeners that he was finished.

When you use a poem, give the name of the author and the name of the book in which it can be found. I learned this the hard way. Once at a series of meetings I used a mighty poor poem as the ending of my speech. I know it was a poor poem because I wrote it, just for this speech ending. The title was "You're a Salesman." I did that talk before four or five groups totaling about two hundred sales managers and salesmen. To my surprise I got over thirty requests for the poem. I had to have it mimeographed for these fans. In the printed piece I gave credit to Anon, who wouldn't mind, I'm sure.

That tailor-made poem was right on the theme of the talk, and the requests for copies indicated that my point got over.

General Douglas MacArthur's ending of his speech to Congress after he was called back from Tokyo was an example of this type of ending. And you know how well it ended his talk. Few listeners will remember much that was said in the body of that speech, but most of the listeners will remember "Old soldiers never die, they simply fade away." The line, taken from an old ballad, gave just the right touch. A similar forgotten bit of poetry might do the same for you.

When you read a bit of poetry to a group, make sure the listeners know you are reciting poetry. One way to do this is to say, "I am going to read a poem." Then take a card from your pocket, and read the poem or verse. You may say, "But it is only four lines. I can memorize that." Of course you can, but the card is for effect. It makes the verse more important. It shows that you have changed from prose to verse.

Another ending that goes well is one in which some action of yours definitely tells the audience that you are ended. You can simply sit down, but many speakers stand there helplessly for an instant and then mumble, "Thank you." The other night I saw a speaker tear up his notes. He said, "I'm finished; and since this speech wasn't too good, I'm not going to use it again. I'll tear up these notes so I won't be tempted." Slowly, he tore up his notes. The stunt got applause, and while the group was applauding he sat down.

I happened to be sitting where I could see that the notes he tore up were not the ones he used. It was a good stunt. It showed he was finished and it wound up the speech. I have seen speakers throw away their notes, and once I saw a man set his on fire. A speaker can develop some such stunt as a sort of trade-mark.

If you took off your coat to start, you might put it back on to show you are finished. I saw a speaker do this not long ago. He said, "When I started this speech, I took off my coat. Now I'm finished, I'm going to put it back on again." He picked up his coat and started to put it on. The applause started. He held up his hand for silence. "Wait a minute," he said. "I'm not finished until I get this coat on and the last button buttoned." He continued putting on his coat, and when he finished the last button, he said, "Now." I found out later that he ends all of his talks like this. For him it is a sort of trade-mark.

A man with such an ending doesn't have to worry about getting a new one for each speech. When he comes to the end, he goes into his routine.

One of my associates told me, "Ed, I always feel that my ending is weak when I depend on words. A little action gives me confidence." It is easy to see how action can help any speaker. The listeners do not expect action; it comes as a surprise. Listeners like action and they like surprise. So why not capitalize on both?

With an ending that depends on words, a speaker is sometimes inclined to rush. He feels that the audience is tired of him; still he has this problem—he must stay in control until he sits down.

When you use a stunt, rehearse it; do it slowly. Follow all the rules for stunts given in Chap. 10.

The anecdote is good material for an ending. If you want your audience to do something, use a story that illustrates what or why or how. Let's say you want the group to contribute to the Children's Home. Then why not wind up with a story about little Tommy, one of the boys in the home? Fill it with the pathos of

Tommy's case. Dampen those eyes; bring up the tears. You have heard speakers do this. You can, too, with practice.

Then there is the speech story that has no purpose but to end the speech. It might even be humorous. You have no doubt heard the story about poor old Mrs. Dunn in Ireland who went to see a young lad who was leaving to make his fortune in America. She said, "My son Tommy went to America five years ago. I had one letter from him, not a word since. All I know is that he lives in a small house in Pennsylvania."

"What kind of a house?" the boy asked.

"It must be a little glass house," the old lady said. "He wrote about how small it was and about the windows. You can see out on every side."

"A little glass house in Pennsylvania," the young man said. "All right, I'll look him up and tell him to write a letter to you."

Well, the young man went to America, and as he rode through the country on his way to the Middle West where he had a job, he thought of Mrs. Dunn and her son who hadn't written. In time he came to the state of Pennsylvania, and the boy kept looking out of the car windows hoping that he would see a glass house in which the son might live. Somewhere on the Turnpike the car stopped at a gas station. The lad got out and went inside. In one corner of the station there was a telephone booth. The boy's eyes popped. Here was the little glass house with windows on all sides and, better still, there was a man in it. He moved closer. The fellow looked as if he might be Irish. What's more, just at that instant the man opened the door and stepped out.

"Are you Dunn?" the boy asked.

"Yes," said the man.

"Well," the boy said, "why the heck don't you write a letter to your poor old mother in Ireland?"

I heard a speaker use that story not long ago. When the laugh had died out, he said, "Well, gentlemen, I'm done, too." Then he sat down.

Here's a story a home economist, Mary Frances Hosmer, used for the ending of her meeting. She had done a wonderful job of preparing, cooking, and arranging her food. She had made a display of it. Now she came to the point where she needed an ending.

"You know," she said, "I was doing one of these meetings the other day, and after it a lady from out in the country came up to me and asked, 'How did you get your job?'

" 'How did I get my job?' I asked. 'What do you mean by that?' I wondered why this old lady should come up and ask me such a question.

" 'Well, I've got a young daughter seventeen years of age. I'm kinda thinking ahead for a job for her. She's too young to be married, she's not pretty enough to be a clerk in a dime store, and she's not smart enough to be a teacher. You've got the kind of job that would just about fit her.' "

That story got a big laugh. It made a fine ending for the demonstration.

I like to end my talks with a bit of audience participation. In Chap. 11 I described how I wake up the audience for the ending. I try to use that ending, with variations, in all my speeches. I find that it works well with all kinds of groups; I have used it with schoolteachers, schoolchildren, salespeople, sales managers, executives, and club-men and club-women.

I use a variation of this stunt in my speech "How to Get Better." I get the audience to recite this line, "When I stop getting better, I stop being good." I ask them to do it three times with me. Then I ask them to look at one another. Finally I ask them to stand up, hold their hands above their heads, wiggle their fingers, and recite it three times again. That gets quite involved, and perhaps only an expert at this participation business should attempt it. I don't believe that this elaborate ending is more effective than the one described in Chap. 11, but I use it to make the audience remember the slogan. Actually, audience participation should be as simple as possible, particularly your first attempts.

Some time ago I saw a speaker finish with this. He asked those in the audience with bow ties to untie them; he asked those with four-in-hands to pull them out of their vests. When every listener had complied, he said, "Now, gentlemen, I am going to tell you why I did that. I have finished my talk. I am going to sit down. If I don't get any applause, I will know it is not because you dislike my remarks, but because you are busy getting your neckties organized again."

You know that he got his applause before the group took up the job of getting those neckties fixed up.

Too few speakers plan their endings. In my book *How to Write a Speech,* I suggest that you write the end of your speech first. Thus you give the ending some thought before you have used all your good material in the first part of the talk.

Learn to sneak up on the listeners with your ending. Don't say, "Finally . . ." or "In conclusion. . . ." I gave this advice in a speech not long ago, and a fellow said, "Mr. Hegarty, you are wrong in that. The other night I was listening to a speaker and when he said, 'In conclusion,' I heaved a sigh of relief."

"Did he stop then?" I asked.

"No, he went on for about ten more minutes," the fellow said. "It was awful."

You don't need to warn the audience that you are about to end. Bring on your ending, deliver it, and sit down.

If the speaker mentioned above had not warned the audience that he was about to end, the listeners might not have resented those last ten minutes. Try to avoid all such references as "I have one more thing" or "My time is about up." Those problems are yours, not the listeners'.

Now let's review the suggestions for a good ending.

1. Tie your ending into your objective. Make it further what you are trying to do.
2. Use your ending to sum up the points you made.
3. Develop a three-point ending. Three steps in any formula or plan are enough. Get into the habit of developing three-step endings for both the planned and extemporaneous speech.
4. Give your ending some order; order tells the audience you have thought through your plan.

5. Let your ending assign the job. Let the listeners say, "He told us what he wanted us to do in as few words as possible."
6. Your ending might offer a plan. Don't leave your listeners with a hodgepodge of generalities.
7. Your ending could repeat the premise that you are making.
8. The formula is a sure-fire ending. Give them a simple formula, and you can be sure they will understand.
9. Try your hand at a novelty ending; see what you can do with a poem.
10. Work out a stunt to help you finish; tear up your notes, etc.
11. Try a bit of audience participation; get the listeners to help you finish.
12. Sneak up on the audience with your ending. Don't let them suspect that you are almost through.

Last night I was listening to the fights on the radio. As the boys came out for the tenth and final round, one of them had quite a lead on points. But the boy who was beaten came out like a tiger. He knew he had to land a haymaker in that round or lose the fight; so he went all out to batter his opponent into a helpless pulp. Approach your speech ending in this spirit. Put on a little more steam. Perhaps you have been good up to now; that's fine—but get a little better. If you have been fighting a losing battle, this is your last chance to make a good impression. So go to it; give it all you've got. Use all the tricks you know. Your ending can make or break your speech.

17

Testing Your Material

A speech is made up of bits of material. An anecdote here, a bit of news there, a stunt, a bit of dramatics—add them together and you have a speech. And because a speech is made up of these bits, it is an easy job to test your material. Perhaps you can't test all of it, but you can test enough of the bits to see what you have before you do it before an audience.

"What can a test show?" you may ask. You can get an answer to almost any question you have about your material. Are your stories good? Do they make the point? Do they explain? Does the listener understand? Does he agree? Is he ready to argue about the points you make? Let's say you have an idea to sell. You explain to a friend why he should buy that idea. He gives you his opinion. Perhaps he buys without argument. Perhaps he has questions. All this tells you things you want to know.

There are a number of tests that the experienced speaker uses. Here are some of them:

Check the material in conversation. Does it hold interest? Does it seem to explain?

Explain the theory you plan to expound in the speech to a friend or to a group. Does it start an argument or does it do what you want it to do?

Have a friend or associate read what you plan to say and give you an opinion. It is even better to have a number of persons read the script; one opinion may not be enough.

Give the speech to your wife and children. They are on your side and their opinions might help.

Get a group together, and deliver the speech to them just as you would to an audience.

Say the speech into a recorder, and play it back.

If it is a speech that is to be done a number of times, do it once and make whatever changes are necessary.

Let's discuss each of these plans.

1. Check the Material in Conversation

Books are written on how to be a brilliant conversationalist. Has it occurred to you that this speech material you have is appropriate chaff for keeping a conversation alive? All right, try it with the boys at lunch or before the bridge club on Saturday night. This will give you some practice and some idea of how it goes over. If the boys argue, you can assume that the audience might argue. If you get questions, perhaps you should expand the thought to answer the questions. If you get neither, you may want to discard the ideas entirely.

By talking out the idea with your seat companion on the five-fifteen, you clarify it in your own mind. Then, too, he may contribute. Many times when I discussed speech ideas with others, I have been told, "Not only that, but. . . ." The listeners have then gone on to add other arguments to mine. I get not only agreement but help that strengthens my original presentation. Sometimes listeners tell me that I am all wet and explain why they think so. This, too, is good, because it tells me that I am not making myself clear.

It is good to discuss your speech ideas with others who are interested in the same cause. If they are interested, they, too, have been thinking about the subject and can offer suggestions that will make your story better.

2. Have Others Listen to Your Speech

To do this, you have to explain what you are trying to do, and that makes for complications. Not everybody is competent to give you helpful criticism. Yet, because you asked them, they feel called upon to give you advice. "It's good, but . . . ," they say. With a group of others I listened to a proposed talk not long ago. The talk was good; it made its points and told the story in an orderly fashion. But you should have heard the comments. Courteously the speaker made notes of all the comments and thanked the critics. When the others had gone, he said to me, "It must not have been so good. They sure tore into it."

"That they did," I agreed, "but if I were you I wouldn't change it."

"You wouldn't?"

"Not a word. I'd give it just as you did this morning."

I meant that, too. The critics meant well, but I doubted their competence.

When you use such critics and one of them asks you to make a change, repeat what you said and ask, "Would this change of yours make an improvement?"

Many times he will have to agree that it will not. When you help him analyze his criticism, or let him analyze it, he loses some of his enthusiasm for his suggested changes.

One good feature of getting others to listen to you is that you get experience in presenting the material to a group. It is like a dress rehearsal.

3. Have Another Read the Speech to You

This gives you some idea of how your talk sounds to others. Reading, of course, will not always give the right effect, for there is a knack to reading that many speakers do not have. Still, if as you listen you imagine you are speaking the words, you will get some idea of how you may sound. In this type of test you have to remember that the man is reading your words, not his words; your ideas, not his ideas. It is logical to assume that you could do them better. If your speaker stumbles over some of the words or slows up at certain points, stop him and ask him what he means. If you find that he does not understand the idea when he reads it, you can assume you have not made it clear enough for the listeners to understand. You are checking for more than sound; you want to be sure your audience will understand you when you speak this piece.

4. Try It on Your Wife and Children

If you are not equipped with a family, try it on the girl friend or the folks at home.

Your ever-loving wife will always give you her opinion. She knows that this effort is important to you, that you want to be good. She will be honest with you and will try to help. An associate may approve an effort that is not too good, but the little lady is not like that.

Your children may not like the piece unless it is as funny as their favorite radio or TV comedian, but if they are of high-school age they will listen. If such youngsters think you have something, you are in. My greatest compliment came from my nineteen-year-old son who listened to me give a forty-minute speech and said, "Pop, that was good." Yes, there are compensations in testing your effort on the family.

When you ask your wife for her opinion, take it like a man and not a husband. If she says she doesn't think it hits the mark, she is telling you the truth as far as she knows. Your employees may "yes" you on all points. The boss may approve the piece because he thinks it is the best you can do. But your wife—she is likely to say what she thinks. When she does, don't fly off the handle. Tell her you thought it was a bit sour, thank her, and see what you can do to strengthen the points she picks on. Most of the time you will find you can do much better.

5. When Checking, Don't Read

When you check the speech before a group of critics, don't read it. Many times I have been asked to be one of a group to listen to a man rehearse a speech. He gets the group together, shows his manuscript, and says, "I haven't memorized this yet; so I'll read it. It will be about the same." That is never true. It will not be about the same. If you have written your speech, make an outline of your points and talk from that. You may miss some of the points, but in working from the outline you will give your listeners a better idea of what you have. For you will be doing a speech, not a reading. A speech that speaks well seldom reads well. So much is lost in a reading: the speaker goes too fast; he doesn't pause; he lapses into a monotone; he doesn't use gestures. Working from an outline, you can get away from these faults and can give your critics a better performance.

6. Make a Recording

Another way to get a slant on what you have is to make a recording of the speech. Set up a recorder—wire, tape, or record—and talk into the microphone. Usually, when you play back your effort, you will say, "I sure can do better than that." And true enough, you can.

Your playback will show you some other faults. You will realize that the radio announcer does not have a soft job. But console yourself with the thought that your speech was not written to be talked into a microphone. The script that is given to the radio announcer gives him time to breathe. Your script is not written with the proper spacing for breathing. Consequently, you will get wheezes in your playback that will discourage you. And the sound of your voice may startle you.

Perhaps you have watched the narrator do the sound track for a movie or a sound slide film. You thought anybody could do it. But don't kid yourself. Talking into a recorder is a job for a professional. On one occasion I had written the script for the sound track for a short movie and we were discussing the narrator who would do it.

"Why don't you narrate it?" the producer asked. "You know what you want."

"Sure, I know what I want," I agreed, "but I can't do it well enough."

The group argued that I could, and just to prove my point I did a recording. I did the best I knew how, but when the record was played back, I asked, "See what I mean?"

They did. I said the words. I got the emphasis in the right places, but I had trouble with my breathing. I was wheezing throughout the ten minutes.

And that is what you will do in your recording. But you can discount that. Your playback will tell you what you have in the way of material. More and more the recorder is coming to be a handy helper to the speaker. Once you hear a talk played back, you realize how much better you can do it. And that is good discipline. You should be dissatisfied with any part of your talk until you are certain it is as good as it can be made.

The recording will show up any faults in your pronunciation; you may be surprised at how you say only half of some words. A salesman who sold refrigerators was chopping off the word "refrigerator" in a rehearsal. He said "refrigeror," missed the "t" altogether. He wouldn't believe he did this until we got him to record a few paragraphs. Then he said, "I make my living selling them, but I can't pronounce them." The recorder will show you that you are going too fast, that you speak at the same pace when you should change, and that you can better your timing. Try one and you will see how much help it can be.

7. Give the Talk Before One of the Service Clubs

You might test the talk before one of the local service clubs. If you hesitate to try a home-town club, sneak off to one of the nearby towns. These clubs are on the lookout for speakers, and you can usually get a spot. Talking before a live audience is the best test of all.

8. Keep Continually at It

Any kind of testing makes you more familiar with the material you use. The first time you talk about a fact, it may seem strange to you. Talk about it three or four times, and you are more familiar with it. Discuss it ten times, and you talk like an expert on the subject. But test your material. As soon as you think of an idea as speech material, start testing it. Revise or revamp according to what the tests show. But keep on testing. A speech thoroughly tested is a good speech.

Here again are the suggestions as to how you can test speech material:

1. Use the ideas in conversation. As soon as you get the idea, start testing it. If it goes over, use it. If it needs revisions, do what is necessary.
2. Explain your theory to one or a group. Perhaps the idea is too big for a conversational bit. Then get a group together, and explain it.
3. Have someone listen while you give a part of the talk, and ask for opinions. Get the junior executives and the office boys. Watch that you don't get "yes" men.
4. Have another read the speech while you listen. The other fellow reading will give you some idea of what you've got.
5. Try it out on your wife and children. You have made them suffer before. Do it again this way with malice aforethought. You know that they are for you. They want you to be good.
6. Get a group of the men who are to hear the speech—a committee of the association—and go over the speech with them. Check to see what they think.
7. In any of these checks before groups try to talk from notes, or without notes, but don't read. You have to be good to make a speech reading sound half as good as the speech is.
8. Try putting the speech on a recorder. Your playback will give you some idea of what you have. It might inspire you to do better.
9. Do the speech before one of the local service clubs.

Testing can help make your speech better. So test at every opportunity—bits, units, or the whole speech. Your efforts at speaking will be better for the testing.

18

What Is the Best Way to Handle Notes?

Why not leave them home? That is a good idea, but there may come a time when you are up there on the platform and your mind goes blank. What then? In such a spot you would want something to refer to, some notes to get you back on the track.

Now any notes you have should be easy to read. Not long ago I appeared at a luncheon with my notes in blue pencil. They were neatly done, in type that was large enough, but the light on the lectern was not working and I couldn't see the notes without bending over. To make it worse, I was trying out a new talk. From here on in, my notes will be done in black ink. And I'll check on that light, too, in time to send for an electrician.

For some reason, listeners worry about a speaker's notes, and it is well to have them hidden. You discourage an audience when you show a deck of cards, or a manuscript, or a folder. They think, "This man is going to talk forever," even before you have said a word.

What can you do? Let's examine some of the do's and don't's of notes.

1. Plan How You Will Handle Them

You have these things to worry about:

Where will you place them?
How will you hold them?
How will you get rid of them?

Each meeting room is different. There may be a lectern at the speaker's table. You may talk from a stage with no table. Usually, if you arrive early, you can get the kind of setup you want for your notes. Let's say you are to talk from a stage and there is no table on the stage. If you want a table, the group will find one for you. Don't hold your notes in your hand if you can help it. With notes in your hand, the audience is too conscious of the fact that you have those notes.

When you use manuscript pages, you have the problem of getting rid of the pages as you finish with them. The listeners are glad to see them go, but the movement bothers them and makes them conscious of the notes, perhaps at the expense of your points. Some time ago I saw a speaker practicing getting his notes out of the way. He planned to read a speech. He had his manuscript on a lectern at a head table, and he was practicing sliding off the top page and putting it on the table. Later, when he read the speech, he did it smoothly. I'm sure that his practice helped. You have seen the speaker who attempts to lay one of his manuscript pages on the table; it slips to the floor and immediately two or three of the brothers attempt to retrieve it for him.

2. Notes on Cards

Too many speakers use cards. You have seen the speaker with his cards clasped firmly in his two hands in front of his ample vest. He covers a point, steals a glance at his cards, smiles a bit, and goes on to the next point. As he covers each point, he slips the card that has given him his cue onto the bottom of the pack. The listeners watch this play with the cards. They hope he has a pinochle deck instead of a full fifty-two card pack. There are three disadvantages in card notes. (1) The audience may pay more attention to the shuffling of the cards than to the message. (2) The cards anchor the speaker's hands; he is not so free to gesture. (3) A speaker may be tempted to have his whole speech typed on the cards.

Even though he has learned his speech, he relies more and more on those notes until finally he is reading the speech from the cards. In one of my speeches, I give an imitation of the fellow who has his entire speech typed on cards. I say, "I have a few notes on these cards to help me remember the important points." I start talking, look at the cards for a point, talk some more, and glance at the cards again. The glances come at shorter intervals, and eventually I am reading from the cards. Listeners have seen this happen so often that the stunt makes a big hit.

There is also the possibility of a speaker shuffling his cards out of order, although in thirty years of listening I have seen that happen only once. The speaker, nervous as most of us are in such a spot, started shuffling his cards. When he came to a point where he needed a reference, he glanced at the card on top and saw that it wasn't what it should be. He shuffled through the cards trying to find the note, and then discarded the pack. From that time on his speech was better.

3. Notes on Pieces of Paper

With your notes on pieces of paper, you are up against the same problems you have with cards. You can't help fumbling with them and giving the audience the impression that you are not well prepared. How many times have you seen the speaker shuffle through his papers as he talks to you? You never know whether he is lost or is trying to leave out parts. In any system of notes you use, try to give the impression that you are organized.

4. Notes on a Large Sheet

The plan I use is to rule off a large sheet in squares and put the notes in large letters on the squares. If I use charts, one square would have the lettering on the charts; the next two or three squares would have notes of what I would say about the chart. The last note would give me a lead as to what to say before I turn to the next chart. I lay my notes flat on the table and the audience does not see them. (These notes are illustrated on page 156.)

5. Notes on the Margin of the Manuscript

Some speakers talk directly from notes on the margin of the manuscript. They use about two-thirds of the width of the typewritten page for the body of the talk and about one-third for the notes. The notes look something like those on p. 159.

A script written like that can serve as notes. You can't help bothering the audience as you shuffle your pages, but your notes are organized and you will do a good job with them.

OUTLINE—HOW TO RUN A SALES MEETING			
1 DEFINITION (1) What it is Group sale Mechanical vs. mental	2 THE ROOM (2) Selecting room Theatre arrangement Entrance Milwaukee Chairs Assistant Chairman–St. Paul Head table	3 VARIETY (3) Vaudeville Ball of fire Pail of water Meetings too much alike 30 days of meetings Keep awake	4 INTEREST (4) The story–Cleveland Gossip–Winchell News–vitamized cooking Language–proverbs Dramatizing People Indian story
7 AUDIENCE (5) Singing–Show of hands–Greeting Repeating a slogan Specific instructions Exercises to awaken them The roaster story	8 COMPETITION (6) Secretary–Waiter Boston story Assistant–Outside the band–The disturbances–Long Branch story Printed matter Samples	6 CHARTS (7) Janitor Covered–Position Light–Spotlight Canton story Studying–Vary the introduction–This is supposed to show Practice	5 FUMBLING (8) Expert–notes–ms–cards–charts Time–Depreciating Apologizing Suspenders Spectacles Leaning on lectern Hunting–Baltimore story–Practice
9 HUMOR (9) Why the funny story is no good Use of story–Relax the audience or speaker Small boy story Memorizing Practice the 3 story idea	10 END (10) Don't let it die out Recess before end Write end first Story of man called on without idea 3 step ending finally in conclusion	1. Train men to put on better mtgs. 2. You'll have better salesmen who sell more goods 3. You'll keep more men working in your factory	

6. Notes over the Typed Manuscript

A speaker friend of mine letters his notes with a blue pencil on the pages of his manuscript. He uses large letters and puts them over the typing. Of course, he then has to turn or shift pages.

7. The String of Notes

Many speakers come to meetings with a list of notes on a sheet of paper. Some of them even cross off each subject as they cover it. Such notes are good in a meeting where certain subjects must be covered by the speaker. They are easy to prepare. Many good talks have been made from notes hurriedly scribbled on the back of an envelope.

8. Get Your Notes Placed Beforehand

You have seen the speaker who walks up to the lectern with a great assembly of papers in his hands. This usually brings the audience to a low point. They say, "Another read speech," and prepare to go into a coma. Perhaps you are proud of that speech and the notes for it. But don't show that pride in public. Keep the manuscript or the notes hidden. I always try to get my notes placed on the lectern before I am introduced. Many times the chairman will do this for me. I also arrange to place my notes under his. I ask him to take his with him. If he forgets to do it, I toss his notes aside. An act, yes, but it seems to the audience that I am throwing my own notes away. They sit up—encouraged.

9. How Much Should the Notes Cover?

In the illustration given on "Keep Them Awake with Variety," one- and two-word notes are used. These are easy to read at a glance. A sentence would be more difficult to read. If you have learned the speech well, a one-line note should be enough. Perhaps you need more, but a note that you have to stop to read is not of much use.

10. Practice from Your Notes

It is a good idea to use only notes in praticing your speech. You will miss some of those bons mots in the written script, but you will gain confidence in your notes. You may say, "I don't know this speech too well." You don't have to if you know the notes. If you can learn to make the speech from a few notes, you will make a better talk.

11. Carry Notes in Either Hand

If you have to carry your notes, don't carry them in one hand all the time. This cramps your style in moving your hands. Carry them first in one hand and then in the other. Then you can use both hands when you need to use them.

12. Watch the Light

Be sure you have enough light to read the notes. Check the light beforehand. How often have you seen the speaker turn this way and that to get enough light to read his notes?

13. Leave the Notes in One Place

Don't pick up your notes and then put them down. Either hold them so you can refer to them or leave them on the table. You worry the audience when you keep picking up and laying down your notes.

14. Don't Place Your Notes Behind You

Don't place your notes behind you where you have to turn your back to the audience to refer to them. If the only available table for your notes is behind you, move it out in front of you, or hold your notes in your hand.

15. Don't Fumble with Your Notes

Don't tell the audience you want to tell them something, and then fumble through your notes to find your reference to it.

16. Don't Talk to Your Notes

How many times have you seen a speaker talk to his notes? That will happen if you make your notes too complete. The more notes you have, the more you will rely on them. If your notes are so complete that you can read from them, and you find yourself reading, use some of the suggestions given in Chap. 23 on reading a speech.

17. Don't Be Afraid of Forgetting

If you forget a point, so what? You know you have forgotten, but the listener does not. If you skip one of your bright sayings, the audience will not miss it, and you alone will know it. Perhaps at home after the talk you will tell yourself, "I forgot to tell them that." But the audience will not lose one bit of sleep over your lapse. It is better to forget a few points than to let the audience know you are worrying about forgetting. So don't worry about forgetting.

A number of suggestions for the form your notes may take have been given here. Try out each, and see which works best for you. Remember, your notes are to help you, not to get in your way or to worry your audience. Use as few as possible, for the more you have, the closer you come to reading. And no audience likes a speech that is read.

NOTES	SCRIPT
Keep Them Awake with Variety	Variety is the spice of life. While your sales meeting isn't a show, you can hold interest better if you put some showmanship into it. No, I don't mean clown it or bring in a lot of extraneous matter just to enliven things. I suggest using a bit of showmanship to get the
Vaudeville	most out of the material you plan to use. In staging a sales meeting, you can take a tip from the vaudeville show. Keep things changing. First they gave you the trained seals, then the acrobats, the song-and-dance team, the soprano, the comedian, the bicycle riders, and so on. If you didn't like the bicycle riders, the chances were that you might like the comedian. If sopranos were no dice, you could enjoy the acrobats.
Stage Setting	And that wasn't the only variety. One act played on the full stage, another in front of a red-plush curtain, and another in front of a drop featuring advertisements of the local merchants. Change, change, change—and you ate it up.

19

How about Some Charts?

The chart is perhaps the most popular speaking aid. It is also the easiest to come by, for you can make the charts yourself with large sheets of paper and a marking crayon, or you can have them made quickly and inexpensively by a card writer.

Listeners like the chart talk. It gives them something to look at; it offers variety; it holds attention. When you show a new chart, you say in effect, "Here, look at this."

The use of charts takes some planning. Here are some points to consider when you plan a chart talk.

What Is the Objective?

Charts can do a number of jobs for you. They can:

1. Help you explain, show figures, graphs, curves, or computations that help you make a point.
2. Give the audience material for notes on such things as prices, discounts, model numbers, plans, and procedures.
3. Serve as a guide for you. You use charts instead of notes.
4. Give your talk word for word.

Those are a few of the jobs charts can do. Each speaker should decide the job he wants them to do; then he should build his charts to do the job assigned.

All Charts Should Be of the Same Kind

Many times you see a set of charts with a number of different types included. One chart is simply a guide to the speaker; another is to help the audience take notes, and a third helps in the explanatory job. It is better if, in one presentation, the charts are of one kind. If one explains, then all the charts should explain, and so on. By mixing types you may confuse your audience.

Material for Charts

Your charts can be made up on cards or on material that folds over on an easel such as paper or cloth. Card charts are all right for a one-time presentation, but if the set is to be used a number of times and carried from place to place, it is better to use material that can be rolled and moved about easily.

Charts Should Be Seen

What you have on your charts should be large enough for the audience to see. Too often the speaker says, "I don't know whether or not you can see this." Then he starts to explain. In this case he might just as well make the explanation without the chart, for such a chart is of no help to the audience. They strain to see for a few minutes, then their attention strays.

Size of Charts

No doubt you have seen speakers trying to handle card charts larger than themselves. For the throw-over type of chart I have found that a size 22 inches wide by 32 inches high is most acceptable. Large or small speakers can handle such charts easily. If this size does not allow you to put all your material on one chart, you can usually break up your material and put it on two or three charts. Many men tell me that this size is too small. "I need something larger," they say. What a speaker wants and what an audience needs may be two different things. Also, if you want to carry your charts from talk to talk, this size is convenient, for it can be rolled into a small package. Larger charts of the throw-over type may be difficult to handle. When large throw-over charts are used, it is well to make them on heavier paper or photographic linen and to bind them with a strip of metal across the bottom.

Size of Type on Charts

Experience shows that charts printed in 3-inch block letters can be seen in any room in which a meeting might be held. I have used as many as nine lines of 3-inch type on a 22- by 32-inch chart. This is crowding the chart to the limit. Four lines are much better. With a large audience you might have to focus some spotlights on the charts. If a set of charts is going to be used in a certain room, it is well to test the charts for visibility in that room.

Speaker's Guide

When the charts are made simply as a guide for the speaker, they need give only enough information to serve as notes. A chart which reads "Interest Them" may mean little to the audience, but it will remind the speaker of what he wants to say about the rules for interesting a group.

Note Charts

If you want a group to make notes, design your charts so that notes giving the same information as is on the charts will be sufficient. Talk long enough for the audience to complete their notes. I've heard members of an audience say, when a speaker turned a chart, "Hold that—I haven't got it written down yet." Brevity helps. The members of the audience feel that it is easy to copy a few words. Make the sentence as brief as possible. The line "Analyze what you have" might be cut to "Analyze." "Cancel inefficient dealers and add on new ones" might be cut to "Cancel; add on." Such a chart would guide the speaker in what he was to say and would also give the audience ample note-making material.

Charts That Help Explain

When a chart is meant to explain, it should do just that. You have probably seen a speaker use a chart that confused rather than helped. At times a chart seems to disagree with the speaker's words. Remember, the point is clear to you, the speaker; you don't need the chart to understand its message. If there is any doubt in your mind whether a chart explains a point, get someone who knows nothing about the subject to listen while you explain it with the aid of the chart. Then have him tell you what you said. Better still, have him use the chart to explain the point to you. Such checking and testing will help you get better charts.

The Chart That Is to Be Read

The chart that is to be read should be written in spoken language. There should be few hyphenated adjectives such as "trouble-free" or "action-packed." Such words read all right in written copy, but speakers don't do too well with them. Words of one syllable will help.

Fewer Points on Charts

If you have a number of points to make on a subject, consider using a first chart listing all the points you are to make. Then use a separate chart for each point (see the example on page 164). If you try to put too much on one chart, you're apt to confuse the audience. One idea to a page and not too many words is a good rule. An experienced speaker soon learns that audiences tire of looking at one thing for a long period of time. They'd rather be shown something new. Make six charts into ten or twelve, and you have a better presentation.

What about Decoration?

If you use any decoration, make sure it is large enough to be seen. The fat woman stooping may be an excellent humorous illustration of the "No Stoop" feature of your product, but if it looks like a floral decoration to the man in the back row, the illustration is useless. Color may be helpful; it makes the chart look better. But does it hinder the explanation? Make your charts as good-looking as possible, but don't clutter them with decoration. Remember, they are to help you explain. A chart done roughly with marking pencil on wrapping paper might be much more useful than one with perfect lettering on white paper but cluttered with curlicues and flourishes in bold colors. The latter may express the artistic flare of the sign painter but may confuse the audience.

Plan for a Chart Talk

Here is a plan I have found helpful in building a chart talk. First, start with a chart that gives the title of your subject. Let's say it is:

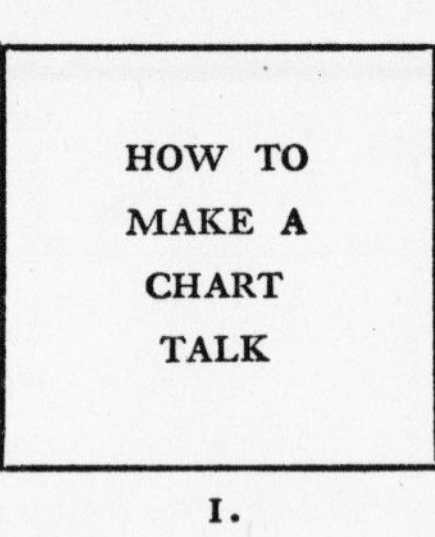

1.

Next, make a chart that lists the points you want to make, like this:

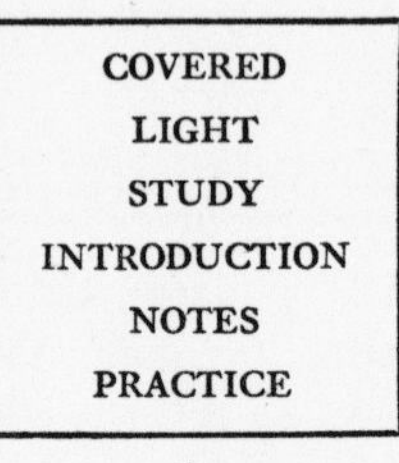

2.

Now make a chart on each point, like this:

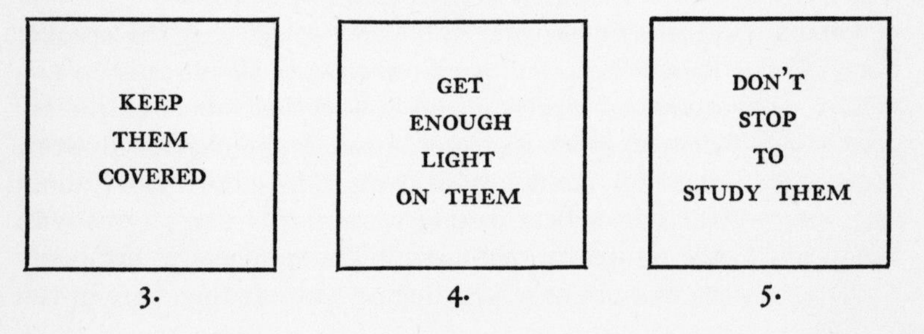

3. 4. 5.

Now you need a summary chart which reads:

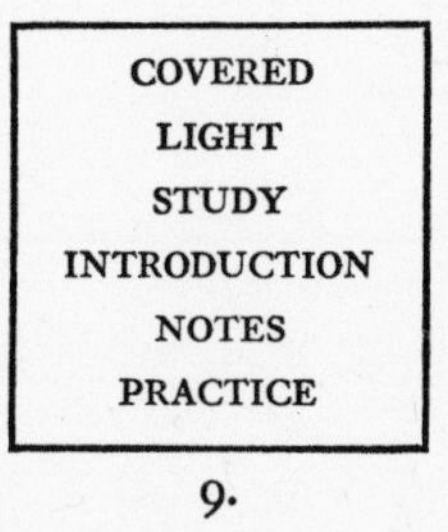

The plan for using this set of charts is this:

CHART 1: *Title.*

CHART 2: *Go Through This Fast.* You are telling them what you are going to tell them. When you show a chart like this, read everything on it. Don't stop to talk about the first point. The audience will read on, and you might as well read ahead of them.

CHART 3: *Keep Them Covered.* You explain that the speaker should keep a chart covered until he is ready to talk about it. You describe how the members of the audience, given a chance to study the chart, will draw their own conclusions from it. You tell a story about the fellow next to you who said, "I don't agree with the figures on that chart." The speaker was not ready to talk about it yet, but he had left the chart in full view. At least one member of the audience studied it and had made up his mind about it.

CHART 4: *Get Enough Light on Them.* You explain how much better an audience can see when the charts have enough light on them. You advise the speakers to bring in spotlights for the charts if there is not enough light in the room. You demonstrate how much better a chart can be seen when you throw a spotlight on it.

CHART 5: *Don't Stop to Study Them.* Remind the group how many times they have seen the speaker turn a chart and then stop to study it. He turns it; he looks at it; he bends closer and studies it. It is as if it is his long-lost Uncle Looie from St. Louis that he hasn't seen for twenty years. Advise the group that when they turn a chart and can't remember what they meant to say about it, to get it out of there quick.

CHART 6: *Don't Use the Same Introduction.* You tell the story about the man you saw who used the same introduction to every chart. He turned the chart and said, "This chart is supposed to show. . . ." He turned a second chart and said, "This chart is supposed to show. . . ." By the time he had done this four times, the audience was saying with him, "This chart is supposed to show. . . ." You explain that a chart needs no introduction. You turn it and start talking about it.

CHART 7: *Put Notes on Them.* You show how you have penciled notes on your charts, notes you can see but the audience cannot see. You say that these worked fine until the doctor equipped you with bifocals and now you can't see them either.

CHART 8: *Practice Using Them.* You talk of the need for practice. You explain that a chart may be turned with a simple flick of the wrist if you know how to flick. You remind them of the speaker turning charts who seemed to be trying to chin himself on them.

CHART 9: *You Sum Up.* Now you tell them what you have told them.

This method of presentation will work well in almost any kind of talk. Let's say you have a talk to do on that fund drive. O.K., list on the first chart all the reasons why I should give. Now make a separate chart for each of those reasons, and sum up by repeating your first chart. In a product presentation make a chart listing the reasons why anybody should buy an electric dishwasher. Now a chart on each of those reasons. Then a chart giving the reasons why it should be your electric dishwasher. Finally, the summary chart.

ORDERING CHARTS

When you give the job to a sign man, make your suggestions as specific as possible. Most of these men are artists at heart, and they may exercise their flair for the artistic on your charts. They have done it to me and have delivered so close to the deadline that I have had to use their creations. They are inclined to make one word larger than another when all words should be the same size. They will give you color when you wanted black and white. If you give them exact instructions about size and color, you will get a better job. I had a set of charts made up to illustrate a talk that had come up suddenly while I was out on a trip. I gave the man exact instructions, but when I came to pick up the charts, they were a riot of color, flourishes, and fleurs-de-lis. To avoid this when you order your charts, cover the following points:

1. Is all the lettering to be the same size? If one line is to be larger, explain which.
2. Do you want color? What color, and where?
3. How about decoration, and how much space can you allow for it?
4. How about illustration? What's it to be, a line drawing or cartoon?
5. What about layout? Make a layout for the sign painter if

you can. It might be well to have him make layouts and submit them to you for approval.

Cardboard versus Paper

When your charts are large, it is better to use paper than cardboard. The large cardboard chart is difficult to handle, and it buckles unless it is braced. If your charts are to be used a number of times, you might have them made on cloth or photographic linen.

Here is a summary of suggestions for the chart talk:

1. Decide what you want the charts to do, and then plan them so that they do that job.
2. Make the charts of the same kind, size, and lettering. Uniformity prevents confusion.
3. Select the material for the job—paper, cardboard, or cloth.
4. Charts must be seen. Have all lettering large enough so that each listener can see it in the room in which the chart is to be used.
5. Don't try to cover too much on one chart; break the data up into a number of charts. The number of charts doesn't bother the audience.
6. Use as few words as possible on a chart, so that the lettering can be larger.
7. In organizing a chart talk, follow the plan suggested: let the first chart tell what you are going to tell, then use a single chart on each point, and then sum up with a repetition of your first chart to tell them what you have told them.
8. In ordering charts made, be specific. Tell the sign painter exactly what you want.

If you have never made a chart talk, try one. You will be surprised how charts help, even those made with crayon on chart paper. Always, when attention is waning, it is a grand feeling to have that next chart. When you turn it, you say in effect, "Here, fellows, look at this."

20

And Perhaps Some Properties

Let's say you want to use speaking aids in your talk; "properties" the experienced meeting man calls them. Anything you use to illustrate a point might be called a property—a chart, a red necktie, a product, or a silk handkerchief.

"Look, I don't need anything like that," you say. But don't be too hasty. Use anything that will help you make a point. You may say, "Oh, that's for expert speakers—the fellows that are really good." But consider this. One point might be made clearer with a chart, another with a funny hat, and a third with a red necktie. Maybe that expert speaker is good because he uses any item that will help him get over a point.

When you use a property, you give two impressions. The audience sees as well as hears. Just suppose that you are explaining how a speaker can hold the attention of a group of listeners. You take a handkerchief out of your pocket and tie four knots in it, one in each corner. Then you put the handkerchief on your head. You know the audience will watch every move you make. They will hear what you said about holding attention, and your action will give a visual demonstration of how a speaker can hold attention.

A point made in this way makes a stronger impression. Do you think that any of the listeners who saw you do the handkerchief demonstration would forget it? I have done demonstrations like that, and men who have seen me do them have reminded me of them years later. You couldn't imagine a prop simpler than a handkerchief, could you?

Let's say the property you plan to use is an ordinary bow tie. There are a lot of speaking possibilities in a bow tie. You can kid about it, say you wear one because the boss does, and that everybody in the office blossomed out with one after the boss started the fad. You might tell the story about the drunk who staggered into a bar with his bow tie untied. He asked the bartender if anyone there could tie his bow tie; said he couldn't ever tie one of the things. The bartender said he could if the drunk would climb up on the bar and lie on his back. The drunk agreed, climbed up, and lay flat on his back. After the bartender finished, the drunk asked, "Why'd you make me lie down on the bar before you tied my tie?"

"That's the only way I know how to tie them," the bartender said.

"You mean only when a guy's lyin' down?"

"Yeah, I used to be an undertaker."

I have heard that story told many times and it always gets a laugh.

But what about using the bow tie as a prop? If you are wearing one, you might untie it, and then fumblingly try to tie it again. Suppose you want to make the point that directions on a package never quite tell a user what he wants to know. You explain that there were directions for tying a bow tie on the package it came in. Then you take out a little card, read what you are supposed to do first, and try that. Your futile attempts to tie the tie will really focus attention on the point you want to make.

You might ask all the men in the audience wearing bow ties to untie theirs and then lead them in a mass retying of the ties. You might produce one of the kind that is already tied and clips on your collar, one that fastens around the neck with an elastic band, or one with lights. You could work up a number of routines with a bow tie, all humorous, and every one could help you make a point in your speech. You would hold attention, too, for every time you show something, you say in effect, "Look at this."

The use of a property may save time. By showing as you explain, you cut the time needed to explain. Perhaps this is because, with the routine you develop in using the property, you stay on the track.

The property gives you something to hold on to. It helps keep your hands out of your pockets. A speaker who has his hands busy is usually showing more life and animation. If you have to lift a part of a product for all to see, if you take off your coat or mop your forehead with your handkerchief, the listeners know that you are alive and awake.

Throughout this book my advice has been to start with the simplest things, the story that is easiest to tell, the gesture that is easiest to make. That rule applies to properties too. You may have seen and heard Red Motley use his sergeant's whistle, or Cy Burg do his routine with the red neckties, or the late Sam Vining get tangled up in his red suspenders. Those properties are simple, aren't they? Why are such things good? Isn't it because they are familiar? If you want to use properties, you don't have to look too far for them. They are all around you. Your problem is to take a simple thing and work out a routine for its use.

Any property you use should be large enough to be seen and it should be easy to handle. Light is a great help to the audience in seeing what you have to show. The stage in an auditorium usually has footlights that throw light on the speaker. Some speakers object to this light in their eyes; they want to see the audience. Spotlights in an ordinary meeting room do what footlights do in a theater.

If the property is too complicated to be understood, you might just as well leave it home. The audience won't try to figure out what you are doing. Remember, your property is to help you explain. If it requires more explanation than your point, forget it.

The electrical industry was trying to get retailers interested in a gift promotion of small electric appliances. In explaining the plan, I saw one speaker use this simple and effective stunt. He said, "Let's say a husband walks into your store. He says, 'My wedding anniversary is coming up tomorrow and I have to buy a present for my wife. I heard her say she would like to have an electric waffle baker.'

"The retailer says, 'An electric waffle baker? That's fine. Here they are.' The man chooses the one he wants—and what does he start home with? Isn't this it?"

The speaker holds up a fiberboard box. On it are a couple of stamps. One says, "Handle with care" and the other "Fragile." The speaker says, "Isn't that a fine-looking gift to take home for an anniversary present?

"Now, on the other hand, if this retailer were set up for a gift promotion, he would hand the man this."

The speaker holds up a package of the same size beautifully gift-wrapped.

The explanation is effective, isn't it? And it is made more effective by two simple props: one, a box of ordinary cardboard; the other, the same box wrapped as a gift. The two boxes helped make his point without the use of a prop that was too large to be carried around. He could get the boxes anywhere. But who in the group would forget the sales story he gave?

If you decide to use properties, here are some suggestions that come out of experience.

Set up Beforehand

You have seen the speaker who gets ready to show a property and then starts to move tables and chairs to make room for his demonstration. Such confusion detracts from your speech. Try to get everything set up before you start to talk. If you need a table for a stunt, have it placed before you are introduced. If you need the room changed around, have the chairman call a recess and make the change during the intermission. The recess works well when you have large properties to set up or where the speaker before you had such helps and you want them out of the way.

In my talk "How to Run a Meeting," I use a pencil, a small card on which I have some notes, a deck of playing cards, and a circular. I place all these on the table before I am introduced. Then when I need them they are in front of me.

Not long ago I watched a sales representative present his product. After he had finished, I asked, "Why didn't you use that demonstrator?"

"I'd have had to stop right in the middle of the talk and set it up," he said.

"It does a good job," I went on.

"Sure, it does, it's great," he admitted, "but it causes a lot of confusion."

The young man knew one of the rules of speaking that does not seem to bother too many speakers. Perhaps you have seen a speaker stop his meeting to set up a property. He gets the audience to help him move tables and chairs. He borrows a knife to cut a string on one of his packages. By doing such things he loses the attention of the group. You have also seen the speaker who starts hunting for a property. He says, "I had it here a minute ago." The listeners in the front row start helping him hunt; the ones in the second and third rows join in. If he finds the property with or without help, he has lost some respect, for an audience doesn't like a speaker that fumbles. If he does not find the property, the group is disappointed. If you plan to use a property, get it ready to use. Place it where you can find it. The property is to help you explain, not to help you confuse.

Keep All Props under Cover

Always try to hide your aids until you are ready to use them. Recently I saw a speaker walk to the head table when he was introduced. He carried a large box with him. The man next to me asked, "What's he got in the big box?" That is the effect you should try for. Keep your props as a surprise until you are ready to show them.

I have seen salesmen show a new line of products with all the models in full view. I have also heard listeners say, "I don't like them as well as last year's line"—this before the man has explained what he has. If those models had been covered or brought on one at a time, the listener would not have formed an opinion until he was told what the opinion should be. When you show as you explain, you have a chance to talk away any dislikes. You can show the pluses, and always they outweigh the minuses. Give your properties a chance to help you fully by keeping them covered.

Watch Your Position When You Use a Property

When you show a property, get it out in front of you. In building a routine with a property, keep in mind the way you plan to stand when you demonstrate it. All the bow-tie demonstrations suggested are good in this respect, for they are in full view of the audience. You can get in front of your charts or of a machine you plan to demonstrate. The home economist puts a large mirror above her head so that the audience can see what she is doing as she prepares food on a table on the stage. A man demonstrating an electric iron runs the iron under a button on his shirt to show how the edge gets under buttons. If he laid the shirt on a table and tried to show that point, the audience wouldn't see. So watch your position when you demonstrate.

Practice

When you stand before an audience, you are supposed to be an expert. And how do you become an expert? As the champions do, of course—by practice. Every demonstration should be practiced over and over until you can do it with a flick of the wrist. Some time ago I heard a speaker tell an audience, "I have never tried to use this demonstrator before, but they tell me it does a grand job of explaining." After that remark every listener was watching to see if he did the demonstration correctly. As you can imagine, he didn't.

One of my friends has a stunt that he does before groups. He flips his necktie out of his vest, takes a pair of scissors out of his pocket, and fumbles around trying to snip off one end of the tie. You are sure he will cut off his chin or his nose, and that's exactly what he wants you to think. I asked him if he did the routine exactly the same way every time. He admitted that he did.

"How long did you practice it, before you tried it before a group?" I asked.

"Over two months," he said.

He had every part of that stunt worked out, every movement of his hand, every snip of the blades, every movement of his head.

The other day I heard a man complaining about a stunt that didn't come off. "It wasn't very good," he said.

"How long did you practice it?" I asked.

"Practice a simple thing like that?" he said. "I didn't waste any time practicing that!"

Perhaps that no-practice excuse was why the stunt had not come off.

If you plan to do a simple thing like untying your bow tie, try it before a mirror and see how you look doing it. There is no doubt a best way to untie a tie with the greatest dramatic effect. Let's say you tell the audience you are going to untie your bow tie. Do you reach up and grab the ends? No, you give it an effect. You lift your hands in front of your face and brush them together, as if you were brushing dust from them, slowly, like a magician. Now you touch the tie, not to untie it—to straighten it. You say, "Looks nice, doesn't it?" You fix it just so. Now you ask, "Which end shall I pull—the right (point to right) or the left (point to left)." Do this slowly. Now you have all attention on the tie; and you have them in the act, for you asked their advice.

Watch the speaker who does this kind of stunt. He goes through all the motions for dramatic effect—and he has practiced and rehearsed them.

I have mentioned the magician. When you see one billed in a club or a theater, go in and watch him. You can learn a lot from what he does. The fellow who sells the potato peeler or the vegetable cutter in the dime store is another. His demonstration is a show. He knows what he is going to say and how he will say it. He has memorized the words. His gestures and movements are all rehearsed. He tells you what he is going to do, he does it, and explains what he is doing; then he asks what you think of it as he explains what he has done. He says something, does something, asks something; thus he tells his story thrice.

If you want to add such stunts to your speaking skills, study the techniques of these men. They have to be good, for they don't have their audience seated in a meeting room. They must stop shoppers who are on their way somewhere, and hold them.

Here are some don'ts in the use of properties:

Don't Apologize for a Prop or Depreciate It

How many times have you heard a speaker say, "This demonstrator doesn't help explain too well, but I imagine you can get something out of it." Don't admit that your prop doesn't explain. The audience will agree, "It sure doesn't." You have also heard a speaker say, "The lever on this model doesn't work right, but I think you can get the idea." Don't worry the audience with such problems. If you are not sure about the prop but decide to use it, act as if it is the best that can be done.

Don't Drag in Props That Are Not Right

Perhaps you have heard a speaker admit, "This chart was not made to explain this point, but I'll try anyway." If you are not sure that the chart or other prop will illustrate your point, do not use it. If some of the charts in a set are appropriate, use them and forget the others. Don't hunt through a set of charts for the one you want. Don't go back through a set to show a chart you have shown before.

Don't Use Too Many Props

Some speakers make their presentations a jumble by trying to use too many props. A mixture of charts and gadgets can make the presentation a jumble. If one prop will help, use it. If you need more, use them. But don't confuse the audience by using too many.

Here is a summation of the suggestions on properties:

1. Don't think that the property is only for the expert speaker. Perhaps the little stunt you do may be the thing that is remembered.
2. Consider whether or not the prop will help. If it will help, by all means use it.

3. Remember that the property must be seen, the object or the type on the chart must be large enough. Get enough light on it so that it can be seen plainly.
4. It must be understood. Too many speakers use elaborate gadgets that give the speaker two jobs—explaining the point and explaining the property.
5. The property should be easy to handle. You don't want to look awkward before an audience. If the property is to be transported, it must be easy to handle; you may have to get it into taxis or elevators.
6. Set up your property beforehand. Don't break up the meeting or move chairs. Have it ready when you want to use it.
7. Keep the property covered until you are ready to use it. Don't have the group worrying about the property or its message.
8. Practice using properties beforehand, not before the audience.
9. Work out your presentation so that you don't get in front of the property and hide it.
10. Plan your demonstration in detail.
11. Don't use properties that are not right. If you are not sure that the property helps you explain, don't use it.
12. Don't apologize for a property. If it was damaged in shipment, use it without mentioning the damage. The audience wants explanations, not alibis.
13. Don't use too many props. A few are fine, but too many will confuse.

Don't say, "Properties aren't for me." They will help make your speech better and will help you make your points. Use a simple property in your next talk. If that goes well, try something more elaborate. The audience likes presentations with properties. They like you better if you show them as well as tell them.

21

Printed Matter Too?

The speaker says, "We have this little booklet explaining what the donor gets for his money. Be sure to get one of them before you leave." He holds up the booklet for an instant and then throws it on the table. Perhaps you think of that booklet again, but chances are you don't. Yet, if the booklet could help workers get contributions, it deserves a better break. You have no doubt been to meetings where the fund chairman talked overtime, had the banker and the lawyer and the paid workers talk too long, and then gave the booklet that explained the plan of work a quick brush-off like the one quoted above. The workers go away with a pain instead of a plan.

In hundreds of sales meetings I have seen the speaker give the piece of literature short shrift when perhaps it explained the product much better than he did. But since speakers do not know how to handle that piece of literature, they neglect it. So let's examine what can be done to give a piece of printed matter the importance it deserves.

You can

- Read it
- Have the group read it with you
- Refer to something in it—a table of figures, a photograph, a chart, etc.
- Explain a step-by-step method of using it
- Demonstrate how a worker can mark a certain passage in it while the prospective donor watches

Have it enlarged and make a number of charts on it
Discuss the idea behind it—what it is for, why the copy is written as it is
List on a chart a number of ways it can be used

That is an impressive list, isn't it? It is a far cry from the presentation described at the start of the chapter.

When you read a piece, don't depend on the reading alone. Work up a few paragraphs of talking to go with the reading. You know how the average listener likes to listen to a speaker read a long piece! Work out a comment that you want to make on the first paragraph. Read the first paragraph; then look up and make your comment. The comments added to what you read make the reading easier to take and may help explain the points made.

You can get the same effect with questions. Read your paragraph, then ask, "Any questions?" If there are no questions, ask one of the group to explain what you mean.

Let's say you have a piece that you want your workers to read but that, left on their own, they won't read it. O.K., have the group read it in a meeting. Don't let one person do all the reading; call on one for a paragraph and then another. Skip around the room, so that they all have to follow the reading. Have a man in the front row read the first paragraph and a man in the rear read the second. This jumping around will keep all heads alert.

At the start of this reading, ask everybody to keep the place, and explain that you may call on any one at any time. Some listeners read faster than others, and one man will be on page 5 while others are on page 3. I have seen speakers use this method and set up a fine of a quarter to be paid by anybody who can't start reading at the right place. This makes a game out of the reading, and all try to be ready.

By skipping from one to another you are not stuck with a poor reader for long. If one man does not read too well, you can call on another almost as soon as the poor reader indicates he is slowing up the proceedings.

When you talk about the copy in a printed piece, select paragraphs that the worker can use. Here is how I heard a speaker do that not long ago. He read the statement. He said that it would make a good opening in approaching a prospect. He asked the workers if they did not think so, too. When they agreed, he said it might be a good idea for all of them to memorize that statement. Then he said, "Let's start now. I'll count three, then I want each of you to repeat that statement after me. We'll do it three times. Come on, now, one, two, three. . . ."

Study that routine. The man built up that statement until none of them would forget it.

A photograph can be handled in much the same way. I saw a speaker with a photograph of a large punch press in his factory explain it to salesmen in this way. He got them to turn to the photograph in the circular. He asked them to tell him what they saw. As they called off parts, he wrote them on a blackboard. When he finished, he had a most impressive list. Do you think those salesmen would ever see the photograph of that press without thinking of its importance?

A table of figures in a circular may mean a lot to the fund drive, but they may be unintelligible to the worker. If the figures are important, you might work out an explanation that shows their importance. Let's say you have such a table of figures and feel that if the worker could present them, the contributions would be greater. How can you make them important to the worker? This presents a problem, for most listeners do not want to understand figures. They are like the young wife who said, "Oh, yes, we live on a budget to keep peace in the family, but neither of us pay any attention to it."

I saw one speaker who made a chart out of a table of figures. He showed the chart and asked one worker what the figures meant. When the first man explained them, he asked another to do the same.

Another speaker has the group help him work out a problem that uses the figures. Of course, the more the group sees the figures, discusses them, and works with them, the better they understand them. But unless the figures are important, your work with them will be a thankless task.

The other day I saw a speaker show a chart in which he listed five ways his circular could be used. The chart helped him get over his points much better than if he had merely talked about them. I saw another man explain a plan and then ask two workers from the audience to come up and demonstrate how they would do it. One acted as the solicitor, the other as a prospective contributor. Anything you can do to suggest a plan for using printed matter is helpful in giving the printed matter importance.

Most workers do not know how to make the most effective use of printed matter when they hand it out. The other day I heard a speaker say, "Don't just hand this piece of literature to a person. As you hand it to her, take your pencil and mark this paragraph. Say, 'I want you to be sure to read this part.' That way she'll be sure to read it. You can see how much more effective such a plan would be than the usual 'Here's a piece of literature that tells what we are trying to do. When you get a minute, read it.' "

I saw one man build a skit around these two methods. First he had the "here it is" worker demonstrate. Then he had a worker demonstrate the marking technique. Most of his workers left the meeting with the thought that they would try the marking idea. I have seen a speaker put a group through an exercise in marking literature. First, he explained the idea, and then asked for suggestions as to which paragraph in the circular should be marked. When he had the suggestions, he asked each man to mark his circular. Then he asked a few of them to tell what they would say to a prospect when they handed out the piece of literature. Any action like marking helps make the piece seem more important.

I have seen the pages of a booklet blown up to chart size so that the speaker could explain it. I have seen these same pages on lantern slides or strip films. As has been said before, charts help in almost any speech.

Talking about the copy in a circular can be deadly, and a little of it goes a long way. Still, if the group knows some of the thinking that is behind the copy, they may feel more kindly about the circular. If you talk about the copy, don't do too much of it, even though you wrote the piece yourself and are mighty proud of it. I have heard speakers kid the copy in circulars. They take a line like, "The eager, thrifty power . . ." and give it a ride. But that borders on tearing down. If you can't be positive, better let the copy alone.

If you have a number of printed pieces to use in your drive, try to talk about one of them only. Not long ago I heard a speaker talk about the four pieces of literature he had available. After the meeting I asked one of the listeners, "Which of those pieces of literature did you like best?" The man said, "I didn't understand them so well, Ed." If the speaker had explained one piece only, he might have done better. It is the same with plans of use; show one plan of use, not a number of them.

The next time you do a speech, don't neglect that piece of literature with a remark such as, "Here's what we have. . . ." Use one of the devices explained to show its importance. Here they are:

1. You might read the circular to the group. Vary such readings with some remarks of your own.
2. Have the group read it to you. Skip around the room; make a game out of it.
3. When the group is reading, have one man read a paragraph, and have another explain what the paragraph means.
4. Talk about the copy in the piece.
5. Have the group repeat a good phrase in the piece.
6. Discuss the value of certain parts. Ask the listeners what they think and have them explain why.
7. Don't try to explain figures unless they are important. If you have to explain them, check to see how well the group understands them.
8. List on a large chart the ways the circular can be used, and explain each.
9. If the printed piece is organized for use by workers page by page, explain this and show how it should be used by demonstration or a skit.

10. Another skit might show how it answers all the questions a worker might need.
11. You might show how the worker can mark the piece as he gives it to a prospect.
12. Charts of the pages of a circular in large size might help you explain what it covers.
13. Don't spend too much time talking about the copy in a circular; such talk can be interesting only to you.
14. Don't make fun of the copy; it might get a laugh, but it tears down.
15. Don't use too many pieces. One is enough.

You can make any discussion of printed matter interesting. I have kept groups interested for an hour showing them what was in a printed piece and explaining how they could use it. I believe my success was due to the fact that most listeners had not heard a speaker talk interestingly about printed matter. If you have a circular that is important, try dramatizing it a bit. Give literature a break, and it will help your talk.

22

You Will Get Some Competition

No matter where you speak, the gremlins will get after you. In the last year I have made about fifty talks to various groups and I can think of only one or two in which I had no competition. Since you are certain to get it, my advice is to learn what to do about it.

Most speakers don't have the least idea of what to do when an elephant walks onto the stage behind them. Of course, you won't run into many elephants, but you have seen speakers talk on while all sorts of things are happening around them.

In my talk "How to Run a Sales Meeting," I have a chart that reads "Don't Compete with Anything." I learned the message on that chart the hard way. You can't, no matter how good you are, compete with a waiter, a secretary, a chairman, or a head table. When I talk in a room where there is a head table, I move the dignitaries at the table out from behind me. After they are seated in my audience, I explain why I moved them.

I describe how the fellow on the end talks to the man next to him. How the next man draws pictures on the tablecloth. How one of them surely goes to sleep. How another lights a cigarette, and so on. They've all seen this happen in meetings, and the description gets a laugh from the group. The other night a man reminded me of a talk he had heard me do two years before. In describing it to a friend, he said, "This fellow moves the head table out from behind him. He says they bother him when he speaks."

Now, that head table bothers everybody, and so do a lot of other things. Probably the first thing that will bother you is the room arrangement. You might ask, "What has the room arrangement got to do with the effectiveness of my talk?" Well, it can have a lot to do with it.

I was in Houston not long ago to make a talk, and the speakers' platform had been set up close to a door, the only entrance to the room. All through the meeting, people kept coming in through that door. Those people pulled the attention of the audience away from the speaker. They also bothered the audience. My plan, when people came into the room, was to stop until they were in their seats. That gave the audience a chance to watch them, but did not put me in the position of trying to compete with people walking to their seats and looking a bit sheepish because they had come in late.

One thing that you have to remember is that when you're talking to an audience any disturbance is much more interesting than anything you can do or say.

Perhaps you've been at meetings where the chairman sat behind the speaker. Then when the speaker was going full tilt, someone would come up and whisper to the chairman. I had that happen to me not long ago. "What?" you say. "I thought you always got the chairman out from behind you." I did in this case, but it didn't stick. I asked the man to sit out front. He did, but after I started he moved back up behind me. I debated whether or not I would ask him again, this time in public, but decided against it. But when someone came up to whisper to the chairman I stopped talking and looked at them. After a few seconds of quiet, they both realized that I had stopped.

Then the whisperer said to me, "Go right ahead."

I said, "No, you finish your business."

The chairman now said, "Go right ahead."

I stuck to my guns and said, "No, you finish."

I expected one of them to add, "You're not bothering us." When the whisperer finished and went back to his seat, I started to talk again.

Perhaps the chairman and his pal thought, "Who is this guy,

anyway, to be telling us how to run our meeting?" And they may be right. My object in describing the Alphonse and Gaston act is to show how some chairmen don't understand that the speaker should have the spotlight alone.

At another meeting when I started to talk I asked the chairman and the secretary of the group to take seats in the audience. I explained to the audience why I did this, but the minute I finished speaking, both of the brothers climbed back up on the platform. They thought that moving them out was a gag that applied to my speech and not to the next speaker.

Not long ago, while talking in a high school, the janitor, in another part of the building, was trying to find a radio program and turned the program into the loud-speaker in the auditorium. Suddenly, in the middle of my speech, the loud-speaker started to blare out a radio program.

Of course, I had to stop. I waited, with a smile on my face, until someone got the thing silenced. Then I told the audience this: "That demonstration cost me three dollars. I had it put on to illustrate to you what a speaker should do when a thing like that happens. If you noticed, I stopped. Nothing I could do or say would be half as interesting to you as that interruption." Just as I got about that far, the loud-speaker came on again. Again I stopped.

I have had stray dogs get up on the stage with me. All I could do was stop while the chairman tried to catch the dog. There was no sense in talking, for the audience wanted to see if the dog would bite the chairman. I have spoken in churches where small children in the audience would break loose and start running up the aisles. Again the only thing I could do was stop. Stop and join in the fun.

Whenever you get such an interruption—and you will get them—don't get mad. Take it good-naturedly; there's nothing you can do, anyway. Laugh at it, but stop. Don't try to talk over such an interruption.

Many times the position of your audience sets up competition for you. Perhaps you have never realized how much the arrangement of the listeners means in the amount of effort you have to put into a talk.

If you get the listeners seated correctly, you will make a much better talk with much less effort. Seating an audience is usually a job for the association or the committee, but often all they do is rent the hall and pay no attention to the seating.

Try to look over the meeting room before the group gathers. At that time a few words may change arrangements so that you have a better chance to make a good talk.

When you speak to a group, you need what the experts call audience contact. Have you ever noticed how much more comfortable you feel when you stand in front of a group close to those in the front chairs? It's this urge to get closer to the listeners that causes a speaker to want to push the microphone out of the way, to walk to the front of a stage, or even to come down off a stage. The speaker may not know why he tries to get this contact, but he senses that if he gets closer, he will do better. At times a speaker may be able to arrange his listeners so that he gets this contact. Here are some suggestions.

1. Fill up the Front Seats

If the audience isn't in the front seats, ask them to come up and fill them. Here is a procedure to follow in moving parts of an audience. First, figure out which group you want to move and what seats you want them to take. Second, ask the men you want to move to stand up. Wait until they are all on their feet. Third, ask them to march to the empty seats you selected.

When you ask a group to move to fill in empty seats, nobody moves. But, strangely, the same group will stand up without too much coaxing. When they are up, half your job is done. Now you ask them to march, and for some reason they do that, too.

When you move the group and have them seated, explain why you did it. Tell them it is difficult to talk to empty seats. You get no response from chairs. But with human beings in those chairs you get a response that helps you make a better speech. A speaker always is better when his audience is close to him.

Another way to get an audience to fill up the front seats first is to rope off the back seats. Some will crawl under the ropes, but not many. Ushers can help, too, by leading the men down front.

2. Don't Spread the Chairs out Too Wide

If your meeting is in a wide room, the audience may spread out so much that some of them are almost beside you. (A V arrangement is not too bad when you are at the point of the V.) Never set up a meeting so that you have three or four rows the width of the room. This makes it difficult for the audience to see demonstrations, charts, or exhibits. It also bothers you because you have to keep turning from right to left to keep from getting in front of your speaking aids.

3. Watch the U-shaped Table

The U-shaped table is popular with many meetings. One trouble with it is that if the speaker stands at the head of the U and the U is wide, he is talking to a great expanse of carpet rather than to people. Not long ago, I talked at a meeting from a U-shaped table. After it was over a listener said, "You made a fine talk, but do you always work that hard?"

I told him I didn't.

"Then why did you do it tonight?"

"From where I stood, the greatest part of my audience was an Oriental rug," I said.

If you use the U-shaped table, keep the U narrow. Keep it so that the listeners in the center shut out the speaker's view of that carpet.

4. Round Tables for the Banquet

When you have a banquet or club meeting, use round tables. Get the hotel to set them as close together as possible. If there is too much space between the groups, the speaker loses some of his contact with the audience.

5. Beware of the Long Table

Many meetings are set up with long tables, and the speaker is talking to table tops rather than to people. Men who set up meeting rooms this way say, "But I want to give them some facility for writing." That's all right if the tables are not too wide. I know one meeting room that has tables about 18 inches wide. These are satisfactory, but banquet tables of ordinary width are not good for this type of setting.

6. Dodge the Head Table

If possible, don't talk from a head table. Or, if you do, try to move the chairman and secretary out from behind. Anything that these people at the head table do will be much more interesting than what you do or say in your talk. Most of them won't object to moving out when they know why you move them. If the table is too large for moving, try moving your point of speaking to another spot in the room. Place this so that the head table is also a part of your audience.

7. Entrance at Rear

Arrange the room so that the entrance is at the rear of the audience. Many times the tables are set so that the entrance is behind the speaker or at the side. You don't want the audience watching the stragglers coming in. You want their full attention.

8. You Face the Windows, Not the Audience

Place the audience with its back toward the windows. You face the windows. This means that the listeners won't be looking into the light, but at the speaker. Furthermore, you will have the light from the windows on you and the audience can see you and your speaking aids better.

9. Get up on the Platform

Try to raise yourself about a foot above the group if possible. Most head tables are on a dais, and this gives the height that is needed.

All hotels have platforms you can use to give you this lift. It is well to try to get up a bit so that the audience does not have to strain or move to see you as you speak to them.

Many times I have watched a speaker struggle to interest an audience. He has a good speech, good material, but he has to work twice as hard as he should to hold interest. If the room were arranged a bit differently, he would wow them. Making a good speech is hard work. Get the room right, and you cut down that work.

You no doubt have seen the speaker who passes out an object for the group to see. He says, "Here, I'll pass this around for you to look at." Then he goes on talking about his subject. That's not good speaking technique. Maybe you want the group to look at this thing you just described. If you pass it around, you are setting up a disturbance in the room that will compete with what you say. The man who holds the object will speak to the fellow next to him about it. The fellow behind them will look over their shoulders. The fellow in front will turn around. Thus, you have two shows going at once.

You also have seen the fellow who passes out an envelope filled with literature. He says, "Before I get started, I want to make sure that I leave this literature with you."

As soon as he sees that everyone has an envelope, he starts his talk. But he might just as well save his breath, for everybody looks in the envelope to see what he has. I've seen some speakers stop the opening of the envelope by saying, "I don't want you to open these now. I'll tell you later when I want you to open them."

Perhaps he never asks them to open them, but his little instruction has kept them from opening the envelopes and fumbling with the papers while he talks to them.

Another disturbance you set up is when you send an assistant out through the audience to set up a property, a projector, a screen, or to do some other odd job. If you have to set up a projector, call a recess while you do it. If you have something that you want done, get it done while you are not speaking, either before or during a recess.

Many times I have seen a presentation made by two salesmen. The men were equipped with a set of charts, and one man talked about the subject while the other turned the charts. The first fellow could turn his own charts and make a better presentation. If you watch that fellow behind the speaker, he will yawn, light a cigarette, or comb his hair. All of that is more interesting than what the speaker says. The extra man is a saboteur. He is not needed. If you are important enough to rate a helper to turn your charts for you, have him sit down in front of you while you do the turning yourself. Let him start the applause, but don't let him give you competition.

Another type of disturbance you will run into is a member of the audience. Perhaps he's had a little too much to drink and insists on heckling you. I had that happen at an industry meeting at which there were five or six speakers. He'd say, "This guy's no good" or "This guy's lousy." The other speakers burned under his treatment, but did nothing to stop him. I made up my mind that when I started to talk I'd try to quiet the drunk.

As soon as I was introduced, I started talking directly to this individual. When I started, his chin was down about the height of the table top. It lifted a bit as I began to talk to him. By the end of my ten-minute stint I had him sitting erect. When I was finished, he stood up and led the applause.

Now, by concentrating directly on him, I threw all my energy into my talk. I forgot the rest of the audience completely. I said exactly the same thing that I meant to say to everybody else. When it was over, one of my associates said, "Ed, that's the best talk I ever heard you give." I had quieted the drunk, but it had taken a tremendous amount of energy, far more than it would have taken to talk to a group. But by expending that energy my talk had been better.

That's one way to handle that kind of disturbance. Of course, you could look helplessly at the chairman, or appeal to the committee. A drunk is a mighty big load for a speaker to carry.

Another disturber is the fellow who talks to his neighbor all through your talk. A friend told me recently, "Ed, that doesn't bother me. I go right on." Perhaps it doesn't bother you, but how about those listeners close to the talker? The other day at a meeting run by a home economist, two women talked through the whole meeting. They were at the back of the room and they disturbed listeners around them. I've seen speakers stop talking, look at the talkers, and say, "Please." That usually stops them. I've heard other speakers say, "Look, Joe, if you want to talk, come on up. I'd be glad to get down and sit where you are." Such steps are rather rough on the talker, but they do get over the point that you want full attention.

Many times you can stop such talkers by stopping yourself. When they are aware that you have stopped talking, they look up to see what the trouble is. If you look directly at them, they may get the hint.

Another disturbance is the one that comes from outside the room. I've been speaking when parades went by, with bands and everything, on the street below. There is little sense in trying to compete with a band. It can make more noise than you can and can be more entertaining. Sometimes coal is unloaded outside the window of the meeting room. I've run meetings in rooms where the elevated railroad went by the windows, carpenters pounded in the next room, or an orchestra rehearsed down the hall. You will get such breaks, and about all you can do is stop. Sit down, light a cigarette—yes, stop, until the noise is over. Then go on again.

When you are speaking in hotel rooms, waiters can disturb you. Once in a meeting in Boston I had a gag worked on me. While I was speaking at the head table, a waiter, starting at the back of the room, walked up to where I was and took a tray with a water pitcher and glasses from in front of me.

I stopped while he did this and told the audience why I stopped. No sooner had the waiter gone out the door than another came with another tray, pitcher, and glasses and put them on the table before me. Again I stopped while he walked in and out. Then, almost immediately, another waiter walked in, picked up the tray of glasses, and walked out.

The audience got a great kick out of the demonstration. I'm sure this was a gag, put on by my friends in the meeting. But do you think that the men who saw that stunt pulled will ever forget how much competition a waiter can be?

I have been in meetings where an employee of the hotel came up to adjust the microphone I was using. I stopped while he was working. When members of the audience come up to help me with a light on a chart, I stop. I had a fellow do that for me not long ago. I had adjusted the spotlight on a chart before the meeting and moved into different parts of the auditorium to see if the type could be seen. Then when I turned the chart, a busybody in the front row came up to move the spot so that he could see better. All I could do was stop.

While I was speaking to the Jaycees in Alliance, Ohio, a storm came up—thunder, lightning, and sheets of rain. The windows were open, and men rushed to close them. Since I was speaking on how to make a speech, I stopped and explained why I stopped. A storm had helped me prove a point.

Once when I was talking in a sales rally the general chairman of the day stood back under the balcony pointing to the clock. When a speaker came close to his time limit, the chairman waved his arms wildly and pointed at the clock. He was behind the audience where they couldn't see him. But as I watched him during my talk, I was tempted to ask the audience to turn and look at him. What he was doing was much more interesting than anything I could do or say.

As you listen to these things that have happened to me, you may want to say, "Hegarty, if all of those things happened to me, I'd quit this speaking business." Sometimes you might feel that way. But speaking to groups is fun, plenty of fun. Surely, everything happens to you, but if you laugh at it and take it with good nature, it won't hurt you at all. Try to take care of any possible disturbances beforehand, but if a disturbance comes, remember that you can't compete with it. Here again are suggestions:

1. Get the chairman out from behind you. He will move if you ask him to.

2. If you can move out the head table, try it; if not, consider talking from another part of the room so that the group at the head table is a part of your audience.
3. Try to get the best arrangement in the room. If you show up before the meeting starts, you have a chance to make some changes.
4. Get the audience moved into the front seats. Try to get them directly in front of you.
5. If you get a heckler in the audience, try to handle him. If you can't, get the chairman to invite the offending brother out to the bar.
6. If some of the listeners insist on talking, you might try stopping, asking them to pipe down, or asking them to come up front if they have something to say.
7. When you have noise outside or down the hall, stop until somebody does something about the noise. The club should maintain quiet for you.
8. Don't let an assistant work where the audience can see him. No matter what he does he will be more interesting than you.
9. If a waiter or a fellow who adjusts the microphone start working around you, stop until they have finished their stints.

I have found that a speaker's best defense against competition is silence. Stop speaking, and you call attention to the disturbance. If the disturbance can't be cleared up, call it a day. Remember, anything anybody does in view of an audience is much more interesting than you and your speaking.

23

When You MUST Read a Speech

Note that the word is *Must.* Unless you are forced to read, don't. Not so long ago, as I came out of a meeting, one of the men with me commented, "Good meeting, wasn't it?"

"Yeah, but why do all these guys read their speeches?" another said. "This reading gives me a pain."

The reading of a speech pains most listeners. I have a friend who can read from a manuscript so that you forget the typed pages. But this fellow knows how to read a speech. If you are the ordinary speaker, it is better not to read your speech. If you are not too good at speaking, you will be poorer at reading.

Of course, there are times when you may be forced to read a speech. Let's say you have to cover a lot of ground in a short time and you don't want to appear hurried, or that you are presenting a statement of policy or a scientific paper, or that you are substituting for another. Any one of these conditions may be an excuse for reading. But don't read because you are lazy or haven't had time to study the speech.

What do good readers do that sets them apart? Well, here are a few tips from my notebook:

1. Don't Apologize for the Reading

If you have to read, act as if you don't know any better. You are stuck with reading, and so is the audience; remember that they feel just as badly about it as you do. You have heard speakers say, "I'm sorry I have to read this. I did not have time to prepare." Why tell the audience? They will know as soon as you get going. Another stand-by is, "I know you would rather I did not read, but due to circumstances beyond my control. . . ." Forget all such apologies and start reading.

2. Don't Try to Justify the Reading

At a meeting recently I heard a speaker start, "Last week I made a speech. Among my listeners were certain gentlemen of the press. When I read their reports of what I said, I was amazed at the misquotations. This time, to prevent that, I am reading my speech." That remark does not cheer up the listeners. If you were misquoted, so what? Why didn't you give a copy of the speech to the reporters? Sometimes you hear a speaker announce, "I can read this speech because there will be a question-and-answer period afterward." Perhaps you have reasons for reading the speech, but don't bother the audience with them. It doesn't help to remind them that you shouldn't be reading.

3. Read Slowly

Most readers, after the usual formalities, start reading, slowly at first, then faster, faster, faster, until they are going like a bat out of Gehenna, at the end. There is no reason why you should be in such a big hurry to get through. When you read, don't give the impression that you have just so many minutes before you have to catch a train. Even though the chairman of the meeting has cautioned you, "Every minute saved will help." Reading should allow you to cover more in less time, for you won't get off on side issues. But take it easy. One device to slow up your reading is to have the typist put about five periods at the ends of sentences instead of one. Then about twice on a page have her leave about six spaces between paragraphs. Write "slow" in large letters in this space or in the margins. Anybody reading is inclined to speed up. In training salesmen with the use of a recorder, the trainer holds up a card with the word "slow" on it when the salesman speeds up. You won't have anyone to hold up a card, but if you write "slow" in enough places on the manuscript, you will go slower.

4. Watch the Deadly Monotone

Most speakers read in a deadly monotone that lulls the listeners to sleep. Vary your tone as you read; change volume, now a whisper, now a shout. Note this the next time you hear someone read a speech; see how much better you like the reader who gets away from the monotone. Here again you might use notes on your manuscript. Perhaps a red line here, a green one there, to indicate change of tone.

5. Keep Contact with the Audience

The reader of a speech seems to lose contact with the audience. Recently I was in a meeting when the last speaker of the day read his speech. When he started, the hall was filled; when he finished, about half had left. Yet I believe that the speaker was not aware that so many of his listeners had walked out. When you read a speech, try to keep the same contact with the listeners that you would if you were speaking to them. Look up from the manuscript now and then. Look one time to the right, the next to the left, and then to the center. You say, "If I do that I'll lose my place." Yes, you might, but what's wrong with putting your finger on the place? You're not going to gesture with that hand and lose the place. It might be a good idea to memorize the words you plan to say when you look up.

6. Know the Manuscript

Know that script; study it; rehearse its delivery. The radio announcer rehearses his commercials, and he is a professional reader. How much more does the amateur need that rehearsal?

The other night I heard two of my friends read speeches. One read much better than the other. I asked the one who did not do so well, "How much time did you spend studying that script?"

"None at all, Ed," he admitted. "I dictated it, the girl typed it, and I didn't have a chance to look it over."

Reading can do that to you. You feel that if you are to read, your manuscript will hold you up. It won't. After all, any script is paper and words that depend on you for the breath of life.

That brings up another caution: it is well to check the pages to make sure they are in order. You will look funny trying to shuffle the pages after you are introduced. Once I heard a speaker read a page of a speech and then the carbon copy of that page. Apparently, in putting his speech together, he mixed the carbon copy in with the original. He was so intent on his reading and so unconscious of what he was saying that he read the carbon almost to the last line on the page before he realized what he was doing. That is one of the troubles of reading a speech. You concentrate so hard on reading that you aren't aware of the meaning of the words. So check the pages before you start.

If another person wrote the script, there is even more reason for you to study it. If you slip up on this, you may find yourself in the position of the mayor of one of our neighboring towns. Invited to make a speech at the graduation exercises at the high school, he told the principal, "You write the speech for me, and I'll deliver it." Since the mayor was good at reading a speech, the principal wrote the speech he thought the graduates should hear, and gave it to the mayor. The mayor didn't take time to read the script before he was introduced. In the script there was a funny story. The audience laughed at the gag line, but not as enthusiastically as the mayor, who was reading the story for the first time. He was so convulsed that his spectacles fell to the floor and broke into small pieces. Without the spectacles the mayor couldn't see to read, and the principal had to read the balance of the address to the graduates. So if you have a ghost writer, read what he wants you to say before you start reading from his script.

But no matter who wrote the piece, remember this: you can't put fire or enthusiasm into a script with which you are not familiar. So learn it; know its message; know what is important and what secondary. How can you expect your audience to be enthusiastic if you are not steamed up?

7. Turn on the Volume

Try to read louder than you think necessary. If there is a microphone, stand away from it so that you can speak louder. The other day I heard a speaker read a letter. He had been speaking loudly enough for all to hear, but as he started reading his voice dropped. Perhaps that is natural. We seldom read aloud; so we forget to turn on more steam when we read a speech. As has been said before, when you speak louder, you exert more energy, and with that energy goes the ring of conviction.

There you stand, leaning on a lectern, with a microphone before you—what a temptation to speak softly. Note, though, that the expert speech reader does not lean and does not speak softly. He seems to blast out with a bit too much volume, but he sounds sincere, doesn't he?

Some time ago after a talk my neighbor said, "Best speech-reading job I ever heard. You could hear every word. You forgot he was reading."

It was a good job, and the comment was a grand compliment. The speaker had turned on the volume. He was reading a bit louder than he thought necessary.

8. Don't Lean on the Lectern

One of my friends said, "It's too bad they don't put a 'fresh paint' sign on those lecterns before each meeting." Perhaps the man had something. The average speech reader seems to feel that that lectern is a cane or a crutch. He leans on it; hides himself behind it; chins himself on it. That lectern is to support the manuscript, not the speaker. Stand erect behind it, and support your weight on your feet. Keep your hands free so that you can use them to emphasize your points.

9. Show You Are Awake

Use some gestures. Although the lectern hides most of you, your head is free, and your arms and hands. Give out with some looking around, some facial expressions, and some arm-waving. Show that you are alive. Pause now and then in your reading. Look up; stop; smile; show something; take a drink of water. None of these is difficult, is it?

I once saw a gag in which a clothing-store dummy was set up

behind a lectern, a manuscript was put on the table, and a recorder under the lectern. Then the dummy gave a demonstration of how most speakers read their speeches. The stunt got a great laugh. You might remember that dummy when you must read a speech. Try to be as unlike that dummy as possible.

10. Use Parallel Illustrations

Anything you read goes mighty fast. You are seeing the printed page, but the audience is not. If you have an important point, cover it twice. Read it from the script, and then say, "That figure is important. Here in more detail is what it means. . . ." Step aside from the lectern when you say this. You might take a card from your pocket and elaborate on the figure. Any movement that breaks into your reading will be helpful. You must remember that any figure you read is not easy for the listener to grasp. He asks himself, "Was that one million or one billion?" If your figure is important, you can show that it is by emphasizing it with a parallel illustration. Use exhibits to help make the point, and when you get out from behind the lectern, use gestures.

11. Plan Relief Devices

Not long ago I saw a man do an excellent job of reading. It seemed that on every page he had some device to relieve the monotony. On one page a story, on the next a wisecrack, on the next he stepped aside and did a demonstration. Here, I thought, was a grand idea for the man who must read. It takes two minutes to read a double-spaced typewritten page, and a relief about every two minutes might keep the listeners from going to sleep.

12. Stop and Ask a Question

Ask a question now and then, one you seem to want the audience to answer. Ask the question, and then step out from behind the lectern and look at the listeners as if you are waiting for an answer. Note the number that seem to agree. Comment on what you think the answer is; then step back and go on with your reading. You can get this same effect by expressing the same idea twice. Read it, and then step aside and repeat it in different words.

13. Use Exhibits

The man reading a speech seldom shows you anything. Yet an exhibit now and then offers good relief. Hold up a card; show a map; take something out of your pocket and show it. Step over to a chart and explain an idea. If you must read a speech, take along a few things to show. Your reading will be much more lively if you do.

14. Use Speaking Words

Try to get your script into speaking words, words with which you are familiar. If there are certain words that you can't pronounce, cut them out. Every speech that you hear read is written. And most of us write in a language that is not the one we speak. When we speak that written language, we sound stiff and stilted. Here is what I mean. This is a written description of a gadget.

"The easy-action metal trigger is designed to assure even water flow from a spill-proof water container."

Suppose you tried to use that in a speech. You would sound a bit silly, wouldn't you? Try putting that line into your own spoken words and see how much you can improve it.

15. Think of Your Manuscript as a Talk

You hear the speaker say, "my paper" or "my manuscript." Try to think of your speech as a talk, not something written, a piece to be spoken. If you look upon your reading as a speaking job, you will do better.

16. Don't Read for the Proceedings

Not long ago a speaker said, "I have to have this speech typed for the proceedings; so I might as well read it." Don't let any such idea trap you into reading a speech. Get your talk typed up for the book, but don't read because you need a typed copy.

One of my friends uses two separate speeches. He gives the association one for the proceedings, and then gives one that is somewhat similar from the stage. "Nobody has ever questioned it," he says. The man who prints the book wants copy to take up space. He does not worry if the copy is not what you said, word for word.

17. Hide Your Manuscript

Try to get your manuscript placed on the lectern before you come up to talk. How many times have you seen a speaker proudly step up to the lectern, drawing a great sheaf of papers from his pocket. As I pointed out in Chap. 17, that sight always depresses the audience. Listeners see that mass of papers and say, "This brother will be up here for hours." A display of manuscript seems to worry audiences.

There is also the problem of getting rid of the pages after you have read them. But even if the audience sees you turning pages, they won't worry so much about the manuscript if they don't see it in the first place.

18. You Might Joke about It

Not long ago I heard a retiring chairman of a committee do this stunt. He said, "As my swan song I have here a 1,600-word report on what has been done and what I think this club ought to do. Now I'm not going to bore you by reading all of it (a pause)—or would you rather I did that? I can read it, or I can hand it to the secretary and let him include it in his next minutes. But that wouldn't get you out of having to sit and listen to it, would it? So perhaps I should read it. Of course, in this piece there is a lot of blah blah blah about the great opportunity I had in being chairman of this committee. It says here 'It has been an honor and a privilege.' That gives you a general idea of the type of thing. No sense reading the rest. Then I make some specific recommendations. Here are some: 'I think the club should have better food.' Another reads like this, 'I think the bartender should use larger jiggers. . . .' There are fourteen other suggestions here but they might be controversial.

I'm sure you all agree with the two I've read, but you can read the other fourteen in the minutes."

That gives you an idea of what can be done with a reading. A reader might read most of his speech in this light manner, commenting on it as he went along, showing he knew how an audience felt about a speech that was read, but still getting over his points.

Why Isn't the Read Speech Popular?

Why doesn't the audience like the speaker who reads his speech? Well, they have been stung so often. If the man indicates that he is going to read his speech, they realize that they are in for a hard time. They have to listen more intently to a speech that is read. That means more work. And listeners feel that the speaker should do the work, not the audience. Then the speech reader seems so mechanical. Just picture him there—a lectern, light reflected from a pair of spectacles, a splotch of face, and a microphone. Then comes a voice reading, too fast, not loud enough, monotonously.

That picture illustrates the problem. The speech that is read needs life. The radio comedian is after this when he says, "Who writes this stuff, anyway?" The man reading a speech needs a similar relief. Recently I heard the reader of a speech say, "I'll go on when I find the place." Few readers of speeches seem as relaxed as that. Yet the read speech needs such relief. But did you ever hear someone reading a speech stop and say, "This sounded swell when I wrote it, but it doesn't sound so hot now, does it?" That line would go over well, for it would tell the listeners that you knew they didn't like reading.

Some Suggestions for Arranging a Script for Reading

If you are going to read a speech, why not arrange the manuscript so that you will be able to do a better reading job. Here are a few ideas:

Use Dashes as Well as Periods. Put four or five dashes between sentences, like this: ----. It will tend to slow your reading.

Indicate Points That You Would Like to Repeat. Let's say that you want to step away from the mike and repeat a point. O.K., write the script this way: "The moon is made of green cheese. ----REPEAT----The moon is made of green cheese." Write that "REPEAT" in blue pencil in large letters in the script so that you can't miss it.

Write Stage Directions on the Margin. For the more elaborate stunts, write stage directions on the margin of the manuscript. A relief device on each page will add interest.

Use the Large Typewriter. Have the script written on the large typewriter, even on larger sheets. This will help you in reading the speech. Perhaps you can read the large type without spectacles. Light reflecting in spectacles is annoying to the audience.

Mark Places Where You Want to Look Up. Throughout the speech you should look up at certain times. One way to make sure you do this is to underline certain passages with a red pencil. Memorize these passages and when you come to them, look up, say them from memory, and then go back to the reading.

Use a Clean Manuscript. Don't read from a manuscript that you have revised. Have it retyped, clean. Those pencil marks and pen scratchings will throw you every time.

Write on One Side of the Page Only. Don't Bind. Not long ago I saw a speaker reading from a typed manuscript that was bound between two covers. His secretary wanted to do it up nicely, and she had. The speaker had all sorts of trouble with those bound pages. Have the pages free. Take off the clip; take out the staples. Have the typist type it on soft paper, and it won't make so much noise in the microphone.

You may think that reading a speech is easier. It probably is on you, but not on the audience. In asking me to speak to his club, one secretary wrote, "Our club does not like speakers who read their speeches." I can understand that. Few clubs do. A club takes punishment when the average speaker reads. So if you are stuck with reading—if you absolutely *must* read—I repeat, absolutely *must*—try to follow these suggestions.

24

Warming up the Cold Audience

At times when you start speaking, you seem to be among friends; at others the faces staring back at you seem anything but friendly. No doubt you have sat through a warm-up show before a radio broadcast. Its purpose is to get the studio audience in a laughing mood by the time the show goes on the air. The other night I heard a comedian say, "They laughed and laughed, but I thought they would never start." There will be times when you find yourself in that position. The audience seems to be half dead, sitting on its hands, daring you to interest it or to make it laugh.

There are a number of reasons why an audience may be dead when you are called upon to talk to them. The arrangement of the room may have something to do with it. This is covered in Chap. 21. It may be the ventilation. In a room filled with dead air and smoke it is much more difficult to keep an audience alive and alert than it is in one in which there is plenty of fresh air.

You may come late on a long program, when they have been listening for hours. Some chairmen are smart enough to call recesses at regular times throughout the day so that the people in the room are more alert, but when you have a spot at the end of a long program, you should do something to liven up your talk, because it is going to be more difficult to hold interest.

Another factor that may give you trouble is a good speaker ahead of you. I once talked to a famous humorist after he had come down off the stage.

"I don't know what was the matter today," he said. "Those jokes of mine usually get big laughs, but today they didn't score at all."

"It was the speaker ahead of you," I told him.

The speaker ahead of the humorist went in for broad comedy. He had a number of gadgets that fell apart, and he kept the audience convulsed by trying to make a presentation with these properties. When the humorist came on, the audience was weak from laughter and he had a difficult time getting them interested.

Another session that is difficult is one I call the "Bromo-Seltzer" session. You get the audience the first thing in the morning. Perhaps they've been out the night before. Stragglers drift into the hall to steal attention from you. Some speakers say, "I like that early morning spot. The audience is fresh." That may be all right with some groups, but in conventions it is better to dodge the first session in the morning.

All these conditions may make it difficult for you to get started. You will run into such conditions, and it would be well to have some idea as to what you can do about them.

1. Laugh, Laugh, Laugh

The idea of giving the listeners a number of laughs is good. That's the technique used by the radio comedian in his warm-up show. He gets off enough jokes so that the audience is in a laughing mood. I have mentioned one of my friends who tells story after story until he gets the audience relaxed. That's his word for it, but what he is trying to do is get them warmed up. How many stories does he tell? Well, that varies according to the audience. If they are frozen, he needs more stories than if they are lukewarm. In arranging his stories, my friend uses the principle of the build-up. First, he tells a story that normally would get a mild laugh. His next story is one that would get a little better laugh. By the time he is ready to start his prepared talk, he is telling stories that roll the listeners in the aisles. A laughing audience is awake.

2. Try a Stunt

You can always startle a group by doing a stunt as you start to talk. Not long ago I saw a fellow show a chart with a picture of a sour-faced mackerel. It was probably the sorriest looking mackerel ever painted. The speaker said, "This is my old friend 'Sorry Mac.' As I look out over your faces this morning I can see a lot of brothers and sisters of Sorry Mac out there. Look at this picture, please, and analyze just how you feel toward Sorry Mac. Now I am looking at sixty of you, all of you looking about as happy as this fellow here. And so I should feel sixty times worse than you, shouldn't I?" A stunt like that is certain to get a response from the audience. It may need more build-up than I've given it here, but you get the idea. Any such stunt should last long enough to get the group relaxed.

I saw another speaker roll out a large tank labeled "Oxygen" at the start of his talk. He told the audience that they looked dead to him but that he had come equipped. He had brought this tank of oxygen, and any time they looked as if they were about to pass out he would squirt them with some of it. Sounds silly, doesn't it? But the stunt did wake up the group.

I saw another speaker wake up a group in an early morning session with a stunt built around a bottle of Bromo-Seltzer. He had a pitcher of water and a glass placed on a table on the stage. When he was introduced, he showed the bottle. "A lot of you look as if you would like to join me in a shot of this," he said. He spilled some of the powder into the glass. He poured water over the powder. The mixture started to fizz. He set the glass down on the table where the listeners could see it, and started to talk. His manner as he talked indicated that he had forgotten the drink. After a few minutes of talk, he seemed to remember it. But by now it had stopped bubbling. He got the drink ready again, and again started to talk. He went through these motions three times and kept the group awake, watching to see whether or not he would drink it.

Such stunts will wake up a group. They will also serve to needle you. If you start with a good stunt, the audience expects the remainder of your presentation to be as good as that opening. One of the reasons they snap to attention for such a stunt is that they say to themselves, "This fellow is going to be good." Let them down, and they go back into a coma.

3. Use a Stooge

You've seen the speaker who had an assistant break into his act with some monkey business that the audience liked. I have seen speakers have a man in the audience stand up and ask a question. The speaker looks as if the question is bothering him. But the two have a dialogue worked out that gets a number of laughs at the speaker's expense. Every answer the speaker gives to the stooge seems to be wrong. That's one of the requirements of this kind of stunt—the stooge should get the laughs, not the speaker.

You've no doubt seen the speaker who uses the dumb assistant. The assistant comes in at the wrong place and does something. The speaker tries to tell him that this is not the time. The dumb assistant can't seem to understand what he is to do and fumbles around until the audience is hilarious. Then the speaker goes on without any interruption.

Perhaps you've seen the same type of interruption by a carpenter coming in and trying to put up some shelves behind the speaker. The carpenter saws a bit of wood, pounds a few nails, and in all kinds of ways causes an interruption that appeals to the group. Then there are the two workmen who come in with a ladder, get themselves tangled up in it, and almost drop it on the speaker. These types of interruptions help get a man off to a good start. Not long ago I saw a speaker make the statement that a listener was afraid to go to sleep in an audience of this type because he was afraid of losing his shirt. As he said this, a character walked across the stage in his undershirt. He carried a sign that said, "I dozed off." The audience said to itself, "This guy is going to be good. We'd better stay awake."

4. Fumble a Bit

A speaker can get the same kind of reaction by fumbling a bit as he starts. I've seen speakers start once, pretend they've lost their place, and then go on. I've seen speakers indicate that they've brought along the wrong notes or the wrong manuscript. I've seen others lean on the lectern and have the lectern collapse under them. I've seen speakers use notes pasted to charts. They pulled off a note and said, "This note is on the wrong chart, but since I've got it here, I'll tell you about it anyway." All this fumbling could be used as a part of the warm-up. Audiences like to see a man fumble a bit, if they think it's real. After they find out he has done it purposely, they get a great kick out of the fact that he tried to slip something over on them.

5. Audience Participation

Of course you can always get the audience to do something. If an audience is asleep, have it stand up and do some breathing exercises. Have it stand up, raise its arms, and wiggle its fingers. Not long ago I saw a leader at the start of a morning meeting have the audience get up and march around the table ten times. This was morning exercise for the group and tended to have them awake when the first speaker started. The "Good morning" routine I use at the start of meetings, mentioned in Chap. 13, gets the group awake and gives them an idea of the type of thing that is to follow.

The audience goes for this type of warm-up. Remember, they all like to get into the act.

6. Work Harder

You can warm up the listeners with the amount of energy you put into your start. This is perhaps more difficult than any of the other devices listed. I have started off with a cold group and warmed them with the intensity I put into my presentation. I spoke louder; used more gestures; threw charts over instead of turning them gracefully. All these things brought more attention to me. Listeners shook themselves and told themselves, "Better stay awake; this is going to be good."

In any of these warm-up devices, you build up anticipation. If the listeners suspect that you are going to be good, they warm to you. But your promise when you start with a warm-up puts a responsibility on you. You have to live up to it.

Yes, there will be times when you need some kind of warm-up. That audience will be colder than "Sorry Mac," the mackerel described earlier in the chapter. If you can sense this as you start to talk, and do something about it, your best material will not fall flat. You will have them with you, cooperative, and you will give them a better talk.

25

Keeping the Listeners Awake

Not long ago, when I finished a speech, a teacher of public speaking congratulated me. "You had excellent audience contact," he said.

That may be the professional word for what I call "speaking sense." Have you ever noticed how some speakers do not sense that they are putting listeners to sleep, while others seem to know exactly when an audience begins to tire? At the first sign, they reach down into their bag of tricks, and presto, out comes a device that revives that lagging attention.

What are the signs of fatigue? Perspiration shines on the baldheads; graybeards begin to look their age; the fat man in the third row stifles a yawn; one fellow fidgets; the next one loosens his tie; another looks out a window; a head drops in a doze. Notice just one of these signs, and it is time to drop to your knees, raise your hands aloft, and start to pray.

You may say, "But I don't do such stunts." O.K., but do something.

A lawyer trying a case in court noticed that one of the jurors was asleep. He protested to the judge, "I want you to notice, your honor, that one of the jurors is asleep. I request that he be awakened and instructed to stay awake."

The judge looked at the juror and then back at the lawyer. "Counsellor, you put him to sleep," the judge said. "Suppose you wake him up and keep him awake."

That is your position when you speak to a group—it is your

job to keep them awake. What is the best way to bring back interest when it starts to wane? Well, here are a few of the tricks you might use:

1. Turn on more steam.
2. Tell a story.
3. Change your pace.
4. Change your volume—talk louder or softer, shout, whisper.
5. Ask a question and stop as if you want an answer.
6. Stop talking.
7. Give the audience something to do.
8. Show something.
9. Do something.

These devices are all good, but before you can use any of them you have to develop that speaking sense which tells you one of these tricks is needed. In talking about why the speech that is read is seldom good, one of my speaker friends said, "Ed, when a guy's reading, he can't look at the audience. And when you can't see them, how do you know whether or not you are putting them to sleep?"

If you are going to be a good speaker, you have to learn how to watch your audience. You have to see those faces and let the expressions tell you how you are doing. My plan is to pick out four faces, one in center down in front, another at the right side in the third or fourth row, another in about the same relative position on the left, and then one back as far as I can see—it may be in the back, at the rear of the room. Why four places? Too many speakers seem to look at one spot in the audience; by looking over the group you get a better idea of how you are doing.

Another plan I use is this: if the four I have selected seem favorable to me, I switch to others. Usually there is a sourpuss in the group. He dares you to interest him. I try to get that old buddy on my side. If he cracks a smile, I know I am succeeding. By watching the audience I can tell the instant I begin to bore them.

You find that many speakers object to working behind footlights because they can't see the audience well.

Not long ago I spoke in a large hall and suggested that they turn off the footlights while I talked. After the meeting, one of my friends said to me, "You should have had those footlights on. We couldn't see your face." Footlights are a problem in keeping contact with the audience, but even with the lights there is a certain part of the audience you can see. Perhaps that night I would have been better if I had talked with the footlights on, but I wanted to be certain that I could see those listeners. If you can see them and watch them, you know when you are not holding interest.

Speakers have told me, "When I am talking, I am so wrapped up in giving a speech that I don't have time to watch the audience." That is too bad. The speaker who doesn't watch his audience misses a lot of fun. There is always the fellow who looks as if he is mad at you, the one who seems ready to laugh, the brother who seems to have had a hard night, and the chairman and the committee who are worrying about the time you are taking. There are compensations in watching the audience over and above what you gain by audience contact.

You may say, "Hegarty, my speech is laid out. Even if I saw a fellow yawn, I don't think I could change to bring him back to full attention."

If you look at that list of suggestions for bringing back interest on page 212, you will see that every one calls for a change in your manner. One of my friends calls these changes "arousers." "They need a little arousing," he says.

The recess is the best of all arousers when the audience tires, but chairmen seem to shy away from recesses. One chairman told me, "If we call a recess, some of them will not come back." I have always wondered what difference this makes. If a dues-paying member would rather spend his time somewhere else, why not let him? The change and movement of a recess or stretch will bring them back for you. Many times I ask chairmen to call a recess before I go on. You can't always do that, and even with a recess the listeners may tire if you speak more than twenty minutes. Then you have to bring them back by what you do or what you say.

Suppose you are watching your audience and you see a listener yawn. What now? Let's talk about how you might use each of the ten suggestions given on page 24 to bring back attention.

You could turn on more steam. The other day while I was speaking I saw a fat fellow in the third row yawn. He didn't try to cover it; it didn't embarrass him a bit. Immediately I turned on more steam. I talked louder; got more intense. I projected all my energy at combating this man's urge to take a nap. As I did this, I watched my man. In less than a minute he seemed to be giving full attention. By talking louder, throwing more energy into what I was saying, I brought him back. Of course, he was the critical case; but others were tiring, too, and my change in intensity affected them also. I have seen speakers wave their arms, or shout, or throw a light bulb on the floor—and there is my friend who shoots the gun. If you have worn them out with what you are doing, try to work a little harder; the change in you shows them that you are sold on this idea. They wake up to find out why.

Speakers ask me, "What do you mean—turn on more steam?" This involves a number of things: speaking louder, snapping out your words, waving your arms, and putting more pep into your performance. Here is how I can illustrate the point. Speak a paragraph of this speech of yours while you stand still looking at an imaginary audience. Now speak the same paragraph while you walk across your office. You put a little more into the second performance, didn't you? Now speak the same paragraph while you walk, but this time wave your arms and talk louder. You sound more convincing now, don't you? Now stand still and put the same energy into the performance that you did while you walked and waved your arms. See the difference in your performance? I demonstrated this to a young man not long ago, and he said, "It's just like getting mad." If you act as if you are mad about something, the audience wonders why, and they will listen to find out.

The story is a good bet to bring back attention. Next time you see evidence of inattention in an audience, start to tell a story. The effect is like a tonic; even if you are a poor storyteller, the group starts to listen. It does not have to be a story that gets a laugh, although the laugh story is good. If you change a statement about a fact into a story about that fact, you get a similar result. Recently I heard a speaker say, "This material is getting tiresome—I mean it is tiresome to me, so it must be tiresome to you. I think I'd better tell a story."

In Chap. 5 I suggested that you use no such introduction to your stories, but where you need a story as an arouser perhaps the introduction helps. If the group is obviously tired, they might not realize you are telling a story unless you tell them. Say, for example, "I was in Cleveland the other day. I was in Cleveland on business, and to see the ball game too." Drag out the "once upon a time" line, and they understand you have started to tell a story. When you change, you want them to realize that you have changed.

One of my friends says, "I have six stories up my sleeve. These are reserve stories, ones I may not use. When I see interest lagging, I bring out one of them."

"Do you ever have to use the six?" I asked.

"No, I have used four, but usually one or two are enough."

Get a few stories for such emergencies and you are equipped to go to work when ennui sets in.

The change in pace is a good arouser. Let's say you have been listening to a speaker read a speech. You glance around and see that nobody is interested. Then he says, "I would like to depart from my prepared address." What happens? Everybody perks up, don't they? Now the speaker has a different audience, awake, expectant, interested in what he is going to say. If a dead speaker with a dead speech can do that, the trick is worth trying.

You have also seen the speaker who says, "I would like to read this one passage to you." You wake up to listen to that reading. It is the change that gets you; something new has been added.

A change in volume is another good arouser. I have suggested that you talk louder than you think necessary. Exponents of this technique figure, "Morpheus is calling, but I can yell louder than he can." Dropping your voice is sometimes as effective. Once I heard a fellow pretend he had lost his voice. He seemed to have trouble speaking at all. For a few minutes he tried to talk, he asked for a glass of water, he got it, drank, and then his voice was back.

I asked him afterward, "What happened to your voice?"

"Nothing," he replied. "They were going to sleep and that was a gag to wake them up. I should have had a white pill that would fizz when I dropped it into the water."

Next time you hear a speaker shout, check to see if he is shouting to make a point or to get attention back. Make the same check on the whisperer.

I once heard a speaker use a paragraph of double talk when his audience tired on him. Those who were wide awake got it first, and then the drowsy ones. In no time they were all awake, looking at one another, wondering what was coming off. I asked the man if it was much trouble to learn the double talk. "All I know is a couple of paragraphs of it," he said. "But it works, doesn't it?"

The man knew that the change would bring them back. A question can do the same for you, if you make it seem important. The average speaker asks his question and then goes on to answer it. Let's say you ask a question and give it time to sink in. You pause and look at the group, indicating that you expect an answer. Some heads will nod; others will tell you by their expressions where they stand. The sleepers will ask, "What did he say?" But because it is a change you will get attention back.

The full stop is probably one of your best arousers. My stops when I get competition bring back attention to me. I can't hold attention while a waiter is delivering cigars to the fellow beside me at the head table; all eyes are on the cigar transaction. But when I stop, all attention comes back to me. Of course, you are not going to hold them too long with the pause, but you will get attention back. Then is a good time to start that story you had in reserve.

To arouse your listeners, you might ask them to do something. For instance, when you ask a question, call for a show of hands.

Even that simple movement tends to bring back interest. When the audience is quite tired, have them stand up. It is a relief to get off those chairs for a few seconds. Have the group repeat a phrase after you. You might lead them in a song. Listeners like to get into the act, and their participation wakes them up. When you see a yawn, ask the group to do something.

You can show them something. I like the chart talk for this feature. In Chap. 19 I said that every time you show a chart, you say in effect, "Here, look at this." Every new chart means another time when they must give you their attention. To prove this, observe what happens when a speaker's charts can't be seen easily—almost everybody tries to see what he has. Anything you show asks for attention. Take a card out of your pocket or a newspaper clipping; show how your necktie is tailored. If you saw a speaker do any of those stunts, you would watch, wouldn't you? So when they tire, bring them back by showing something.

You can get the same result by doing something. Take off your necktie, and the fellow next to the sleeper nudges the sleeper. "Wake up," he says, "this is going to be good." Not long ago I watched a speaker take a drink of water from a pitcher on the table beside him. He poured the water into the glass slowly, as if he was trying not to spill any. Then he turned his profile to the audience while he took a long drink, again slowly. He took a handkerchief out of his lapel pocket and touched his lips lightly. Then he went back to his talking. I was certain that he didn't need the drink, that it was an act. But during the performance he had every eye on him. I have seen speakers muss their hair, comb their hair, try to tear out their hair, brush their hair down in front of their eyes, all to hold attention or to bring it back. At the sign of a yawn, wake yourself up and do something.

One reason for lack of attention is that the audience can't hear you. Inattention in the rear of the room may warn you of this. If the listeners down front seem awake and those in the rear restless, ask, "Can you hear me back there?" You have to remember that if the group can't hear you, they will not try to listen.

Many times interest in what you are saying wanes because the listeners can't see what you are doing. I have seen speakers do a demonstration of a machine on a stage when half the men in the audience were not able to see the machine or its parts. The type on your charts may be too small. The object you show may be almost invisible. An audience will strain to see for a while, but will soon give up. Recently I was on a program with a man who had forty minutes for his presentation. He finished in fifteen minutes. I asked him why. "They couldn't see a thing I was doing," he said. The speaker was wise. Instead of beating his brains out for his allotted forty minutes, he quit. He knew that he couldn't hold attention if the group couldn't see.

In building a reserve of these arousers, try for variety. Don't rely on stories alone. There are nine devices listed on page 212; why not develop one of each? Some will work for you; others will not. Determine which are for you, and put them into your bag of tricks.

Even when you have a good talk, you may find that listeners tire. Recently, I attended a meeting of our advertising club. The speaker was good, and he handled his subject interestingly; yet I dozed off while he was talking. My associates said, "You say a listener goes to sleep because the speaker is no good. This was a good speaker and you went to sleep on him."

I have tried to analyze why I went to sleep. It was not the subject or the speaker—it was a tired man, at the end of a hard day, breathing secondhand air in a smoke-filled room. That's a handicap for any speaker. But you will have such handicaps, and it will pay you to be prepared for them. Arm yourself with some arousers; they will come in handy.

26

If You Have to Make a Speech Next Week

Not long ago I was in a bookstore in Dallas, Texas, and saw a stack of copies of my book *How to Write a Speech* on a counter. As I was proudly looking through one of them, a saleswoman asked me, "Is there anything I can do for you?" I told her not just then, but asked, "Does anybody ever buy these books on speechmaking?" There were a number of such books on the counter.

"Yes, we sell quite a few of them," she said.

"Why would anybody buy a book like this?" I asked.

"Most of them," she said, "tell me that they have to make a speech tomorrow or next week and they don't know how to do it; so they rush out and buy a book."

Now if you are in that spot, this chapter will help you. It sums up briefly much of what is in this book. If you have to give a speech tomorrow, you won't have time to read the entire book—but go through this chapter, use some of the suggestions, and you will do a bit better. I have brought together a number of suggestions from earlier chapters so that you can read them while you run. For those who have read the entire book, this chapter will serve as a review.

1. Talk Louder

As you start, use more volume than you think you need. Many times when I have been speaking—plenty loud enough, I thought

—a voice at the side or back of the room has called, "Louder, please." When you talk louder, you exert more energy and thus throw more effort into what you say. If you seem steamed up about a subject or a point, the audience feels that it should be interested, too.

2. Get up on a Stage

Always try to be on a level above the audience when you talk. Most head tables are raised a bit. Most lecterns are on a platform. Most association speeches are made from a stage. I have spoken to clubs that use the "no head table" idea. In a large hotel ballroom this is not good unless a raised platform is set up for the speaker. Many times I have had to arrange for this platform myself, but I always try to get it because it puts me up where all can see me. An audience wants to see as well as hear; it is restless when it can't see. What the speaker does usually adds a lot to the talk. His facial expressions, his gestures, and his stunts may be weakened if the audience can't see everything he is doing. Remember, the audience wants to see; therefore speak from a platform.

3. Watch the Faces

Watch the audience. Most speakers seem to forget the audience entirely. If you watch the audience, you can tell when they begin to tire. Keep looking around the room. Look at the faces, not over them. The experts call this "keeping eye contact" with the audience. Remember, a yawn is not the listener's fault; it is your fault. When you see a yawn, do something. Start telling a story, do a stunt, put on more steam—yes, even go into your ending. Too many speakers seem to think only of themselves and their speech. Watch the faces. Let those faces tell you as much as you are telling the listeners.

4. Face the Audience

Keep your face toward the audience. They like to see your facial expressions, to feel that they know you. In conversation with a group you face each of them; try for that effect when you make a speech. You are conversing with them, not talking at them. If you have demonstrations to make or charts to show, plan the showing so that you don't turn your back to the audience for any great length of time. If you must talk when you turn from the audience, raise your voice so that all will hear. Never talk to a property you are using—talk to the audience. If the chairman stays up front, don't turn to talk to him. Talk to the audience always.

5. Stand Still

Once I gave a talk before a group of merchants. The next morning one of the listeners said, "That was a good talk you did last night. But why didn't you stand still. You made me nervous walking up and down on that stage." Why was I walking? Well, I was thinking of me instead of the audience. I was running this meeting and had brought in an outside speaker. He had been completely off the beam and, to add to the confusion, he had stayed on thirty minutes longer than the time allotted him. I came on after him, and in my anxiety to make up time, I talked faster and my walking up and down the stage was closer to running. Try to imagine the feelings of the listeners in the front rows when the speaker moves about. Their heads bob following him. Stand as near one spot as you can. If you must move about because of props, do it slowly.

6. Stand Erect

Don't lean on a lectern, sit on a table, or lean against the wall when you talk. Stand erect, on your own two feet. Don't slouch or assume parade rest. Stand on your toes, lean a bit forward, and give out. It pays to be an eager beaver when you are talking to a group. Give the impression that you are full of energy, raring to go. That attitude is catching.

7. Watch Your Nervous Habits

Don't pull at your ear, scratch your head, rub your nose, or smooth your hair. What can a man say that is more interesting—or annoying—than the spectacle of a man indulging in nervous mannerisms? So watch your nervous habits. Perhaps you hook your fingers in the armholes of your vest when you talk to the boys in the office, but don't do it on a speaker's platform. If it is a stunt, a demonstration, or an imitation, O.K.; otherwise, no. Put all your nervous energy into your speech.

8. Leave Your Spectacles Alone

Put your spectacles on or leave them off, but don't be taking them off and putting them on while you are talking. Don't wave them at the audience or use them in your gestures. In my talk on "How to Make a Speech" I do an imitation of the man who uses his spectacles to threaten the audience. That imitation always get a laugh, for the listeners have seen speaker after speaker use their spectacles for almost everything but an aid to vision.

9. Don't Play with Your Clothes

Don't tug at your necktie, twirl your watch chain, pull up your trousers, or worry about that inside button on your double-breasted suit. When you do such things, you draw the attention of the audience to your clothes.

10. Get Your Suit Pressed

Get your suit pressed before any performance. Wear a suit that sets you off. Your best suit is good if it doesn't look too new. Don't wear trick clothes unless you are selling clothes.

Dress as the group does. If you are to speak from a stage, a double-breasted suit often looks best. If you wear a single-breasted suit, wear suspenders, too; the suspenders will keep your vest and pants from parting company when you make some of your more elaborate gestures. Why should an audience take advice from you if you don't look like an expert?

11. Don't Smoke

How many times have you seen a speaker light a cigarette while talking to an audience? You can't play with a cigarette and talk at the same time. You have to stop to light it; you have to stop to snuff it out. You can't afford to distract the attention of the audience by smoking.

12. Don't Anchor Your Hands

Don't clasp your hands behind you. Don't shove them into your coat pockets. Don't fold your arms either in front or in back of you. Don't hold your elbows. Leave your hands free. In conversation, when you make a point, you instinctively use your hands; it's natural. Why anchor them when you are making a speech? When you keep them in one place, you cut down the energy you put into what you say. If you give your hands a chance, you will use them unconsciously, and any motion adds helpful emphasis to what you say.

13. Don't Use the Same Motion

Don't use the same motion over and over. I have a friend who keeps shaking his finger at the audience all through his speech. When I mentioned this to him, he said, "That's a hang-over from my schoolteaching days." We worked out three other gestures to go with the finger shaking, and now he doesn't give the impression that you must do it his way, or else. If you have only one gesture, develop a few more. Practice them in front of a mirror until you have them perfect. Then use them throughout the speech.

14. Don't Worry about Diction

Don't worry too much about diction—before an audience, that is. If you say "git" for "get" or forget the last "g" in going, let the slip ride. Don't repeat and correct it. If you worry about diction while you are speaking, you may get your ideas all tangled. Once I took a course in speaking, and the instructor gave quite a bit of attention to diction. Since I came from the Middle West, I used what he called the burred "r." I said "togetherr" instead of "togethah." Well, he worked on me to correct that and other faults. One day one of my associates said to me, "You know, this guy's ruining you as a speaker."

"He is?" I asked. "How?"

"He's got you worrying about how you say words, rather than about what you say."

I thought that over and decided that my friend was right. I went back to saying "togetherr," and I believe my speaking improved. If you worry on the platform about diction, it may affect your speaking. Worry about it and practice it at home and then forget about it when you get up to speak.

15. Don't Promise to Cover Something Later

For some reason, speakers feel that an audience is following so closely that it spots a point that has been missed. It is difficult for the average listener to keep up with you, let alone get ahead of you. If you are not covering a point adequately, you will know it, but the audience will not. Many times when a speaker promises to cover a point later he never gets around to it. Don't promise; it is difficult to make good on many of those promises.

16. Don't Mention Time

Time is mentioned in so many ways, and there is so little sense in it. Speakers love to tell the listeners that they don't have time to cover their subject adequately. If you are stuck with the job of covering a thirty-minute subject in ten minutes, it is your problem, not theirs. Remember, the time you mention belongs to the audience. Instead of listening to you they could be listening to the radio or watching television. So don't remind them that you are using their time. Forget time and get on with your speech.

17. Don't Compete with Anything

If someone comes up to speak to the chairman, stop talking until the conversation is finished. If a waiter comes up to the head table, stop talking until he finishes his business. Nothing you do can be as interesting as that waiter changing the pitchers of ice water. The vaudeville actor always mentioned the member of the audience who came in late. He usually got a laugh. But he knew competition when he saw it. Most speakers don't recognize these disturbances, and they talk on. They might do better if they stopped. Focus the attention of the listeners on the disturbance, and chances are the disturbance will be shortened.

18. Don't Set up Competition

Many speakers set up competition for themselves. They pass around an object for the audience to look at while they talk on. They hand out an envelope full of literature. Such actions set up competition for you. No speaker can hold interest against such disturbances. The experienced speaker doesn't set them up.

19. Get Your Back to the Wall

When you speak, try to get your back to a curtain or wall so that nothing behind you can distract the attention of the listeners. Any moving object behind you—a chairman, an assistant, a head table —takes attention from you. Try for an arrangement that focuses attention on you. It is difficult to hold attention with all conditions favorable, so try for the best. Get your back to the wall.

20. Don't Be Stiff and Formal

Unless you are a big shot, don't try to pretend that you are one. Don't step out of character for a minute. Don't doll up your remarks in your Sunday language. Show that you are a regular fellow, a good Joe, one of them.

21. Button up Your Points

When you make a point, tell the listeners what the point is, then bring on your evidence, and then wrap it into a package by telling them again what the point is. Here is where most speakers fail. They present a lot of evidence, but they don't relate it to the point they are making. Follow the formula of the Negro preacher, "First I tells them what I am going to tell them; second, I tells them; and third, I tells them what I done told them."

22. Get a Good Ending

Work out your ending first. Try a simple three-step summation for your windup—first this, then this, and then this. If you have a good ending, you will leave a good impression and perhaps a better idea of what you want them to do.

23. Some Thoughts about the Use of a Microphone

Today at most association meetings the committee will have an amplifying system available for your use. Now microphones and loud-speakers are there for one purpose—to help the audience hear. Without that microphone and amplifier system your words may be lost, at least to a portion of the audience. Some suggestions on the use of microphones follow:

If You Have One, Use It. If the committee has furnished a microphone, use it. Don't be like the professor on a program with me last month. When they told him there was an address system, he said, "Oh, I'll not need that. My voice has volume and it carries. Why, I speak to students every day." Well, his voice had volume, and perhaps it carried, but not in that hall. Persons beyond the third row claimed they had difficulty hearing him. But how could the professor know that this hall had poor acoustics? I made a speech some years ago in a large ballroom of a hotel. Before the meeting, the committee and I decided that we would not use a microphone.

After the talk I asked one of the group, "Could everybody hear?"

"It came over great," he replied.

"Then we didn't need a microphone."

"Yes, we did," he said. "And we had one. It was hidden up there behind the lectern. I was glad we had it."

That microphone was not up in front of my face, but it was doing its job picking up my voice and giving me the extra volume that helped the listeners hear.

If the committee has provided a microphone, use it. They know the hall and its limitations. Rely on their judgment. It pays off in the end.

Don't Fuss with It. If the microphone is on a stand before you on a stage, keep your hands off it. Don't try to adjust it; don't fondle it; don't lean on it. I remember one speaker who kept playing with a little screw on the microphone. Finally, he got the thing apart, one part in one hand, the other in the other. Then the meeting had to stop while the committee looked for the hotel electrician to put the microphone together again. You have seen the speaker who uses the microphone for a crutch, who holds onto it for dear life. Even professional entertainers do that. They are nervous, and they feel they need something to hang on to. Try to get the microphone adjusted before you start to talk. Don't worry if it is an inch or two high or low. Unless it is completely out of adjustment for your height, leave it alone. If an electrician comes up to adjust it while you are speaking, stop speaking until he is out of sight.

Don't Ask If It Is on. You have heard the speaker ask the audience, "Is this thing on?" Don't do that. Check before you get up to talk. If it is not on, the audience will tell you. The committee will do something about it. It is the committee's job, anyway, not yours. You are the guest speaker.

Stand Away and Give Out. Stand back from the microphone and speak in your natural tone of voice. Use about the same volume you would if you had no microphone. Don't hug the microphone and whisper into it. If you have a shouting line, move back a bit before you blast out.

It Helps to Hide the Microphone. If you are running the meetings of a club or association, it may pay you to build a lectern with a hidden microphone. I have such a lectern I use in business meetings. The speaker is told, "We are using a microphone, and if you will talk in a normal tone it will pick up your volume enough so that everybody can hear." With the microphone hidden, the speaker does not worry about it. He resists the urge to adjust it. He speaks in his natural voice, and the man on the control adjusts the volume to the audience.

When the Microphone Isn't Working. Not long ago at a meeting the address system was acting up. It was feeding back with that hum which drives listeners to distraction. Yet in that room the speaker could not be heard without the microphone. In this case the speaker asked, "Would it be better with or without the mike?"

The audience voted to use the microphone, even with the hum. In such a case the best thing to do is to ask the audience. Most groups would rather hear with the hum than not hear without it.

What about Lapel Microphones? Lapel microphones are useful when the speaker has to move about. One disadvantage is that usually there is quite a bit of fumbling when the microphone is passed from the chairman to the speaker. When the speaker touches the microphone, there is a scratching sound that is annoying. I saw this handled almost silently in a meeting not long ago. A man on the controls cut off the microphone while it was being passed from one man to another. When you are using a lapel microphone, don't turn your head too much toward it. If you get too close, you will blast out at the group.

27

Try for the Best Performance

When I was new at this speaking business, an old hand at it gave me this advice, "Every time you speak, try to be the best on the program."

That is good advice for anyone. Never go into a meeting with the thought that another speaker will be better than you are. Make up your mind that you will be the best speaker on the list, and go out on the stage trying to be just that. Such an objective will make you better.

Competition can make you better. Recently I was told that I would be on the program with a speaker who was using a half ton of equipment.

I asked, "Does he use any audience participation?"

"No, it's mainly properties for stunts he does," the chairman replied.

That gave me a clue. I couldn't bring a ton of equipment with me; so I worked out a few audience participation stunts to compete with his big props. I don't know who was better, but even if it was a draw, I know this—he made a big impression with his stunts, and I made a big one with my audience participation.

This gives you an idea of how you should feel about your part on any program. Make it just as good as you can. Nobody can ask for more than that.

You may say, "That fellow is a born talker. I can't hope to compete with him." Perhaps he is, but there is something that you can do better than he can. Try to find that one thing. One of my associates says, "I can talk for fewer minutes." That may be the advantage. But whatever it is, find it and exploit it.

If you want to be a good speaker, there is no reason why you cannot be one. You have heard speakers with every disability—size, voice, presence, personality—yet they were good. They started with those disabilities and overcame them. As you analyze what you have as a speaker, you may find that you too have some negatives in your speaking make-up. With work and practice you can overcome them.

The best way to start is to watch other speakers, and note how they handle material. When a man makes a point well, note how he does it. When a speaker bores a group, note what he does. Study the speech construction of the man who holds an audience spellbound. How did he do it? When you get so that you can analyze a good speaker's stunts, delivery, and gestures, you will find that your own efforts will begin to improve.

One thing to check is the frequency with which good speakers use the devices mentioned in this book. Some use one of the devices and put on a good performance. Others use many of them and are perhaps a bit better. The fact that a man can become expert at using the anecdote and be a good talker because of that one skill should encourage any beginner. Surely you can learn to be good at one of these speaking skills.

But remember this—it helps to have something to say. Dress up that something to say with the suggestions given in this book. Then get up on the stage and give out—loud. Always be trying for that blue ribbon. Try to make the best speech of the lot. If you put all you have into that try, you can't help being good.

You know, any speaker feels good when he hears the applause at the end of his speech. But nothing can equal the thrill of feeling that he deserved it.

Index

J

K

L

M

N

O

P

Q